I0004916

Adobe Photoshop CC (2015): The ultimate Guide for beginners to learn digital Photoshop the easy way

By Mark Klasfield

Adobe Photoshop CC Tutorial

Table of Contents

Lesson 1: Introduction

What is Photoshop?

Photoshop is an image editing application which is used by many professional photographers and designers. It can be used for any kind of image editing so as to transform the snapshots and graphics into images that will take your words to the next level. Photoshop has so many features; hence it is very powerful application. And that also makes it very expensive. It may not be best option for photo/image editing if it is not going to be used professionally.

You can use Photoshop for almost any kind of image editing; such as touching up photos, creating high-quality graphics, and much, much more. In this lesson, we'll introduce you to the Photoshop interface. It includes how to open files, work with panels, customize the workspace, and change the display size.

Photoshop is a complex application and it can feel a bit intimidating to use at first. Because of this, we recommend downloading our example file along with the lesson (right-click the link to save it). The more hands-on experience you have with Photoshop, the easier it will become to use.

Lesson 2: Getting to know the Interface

Opening files

Most of the times, you'll want to start by opening an existing photo rather than creating a new blank image. Photoshop allows you to open and edit existing image files, such as .jpg or .png files, as well as .psd (Photoshop document) files.

To open a file:

1. Select File: Open.

2. A dialog box will appear. Locate and select the file on your computer, then click Open.

3. The file will appear in Photoshop.

If you don't currently have Photoshop open, you can locate and right-click the file on your computer and then choose Open with Adobe Photoshop to open the file.

Overview of the Photoshop interface

As Photoshop is designed primarily for professional use, the interface may feel a bit complex and intimidating for new users. Even if you have some experience with other image editing software, it's a good idea to become familiar with the different parts of the Photoshop interface.

Looking at the image below you can become more familiar with the Photoshop interface.

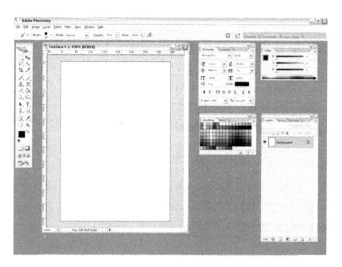

Working with Tools and other panels

The Tools panel

The Tools panel is one of the most important features in Photoshop—it's where you'll select different tools for editing images. Once you've chosen a tool, you'll be able to use it with the current document. Your cursor will change to reflect the currently selected tool.

You can also click and hold to select a different tool. For example, you can click and hold the Rectangle tool to select different Shape tools, such as the Ellipse, Line, or Custom shape tools.

Showing and hiding panels

You'll also be able to view and modify a lot of information about the current document through the other panels in the workspace. For example; you can view the document's layers in the Layers panel. To show or hide any panel, click the Window menu and then select the desired panel—currently visible panels are indicated by a check mark. In the image below, we're using the Window menu to turn on the History panel.

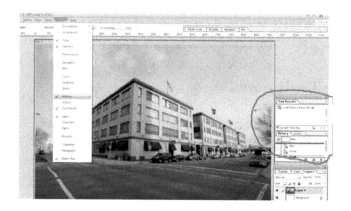

You can use the double-arrows to expand or collapse panels. This can be helpful if you want to temporarily hide a panel without removing it from the workspace.

You can also press the Tab key on your keyboard to show or hide all active panels.

Moving panels

If you want to change a panel's location, you can move it by clicking and dragging the panel to a new part of the workspace.

However, if you're planning to follow along with our tutorial, we recommend keeping most panels in the default location for now. To reset the panels to their default positions, select Window then Workspace: Reset

Essentials. Note that this process may vary depending on which version of Photoshop you're using. For example, in Photoshop Elements, you'll go to Window: Reset Panels.

Customizing the Photoshop environment

If you want to customize Photoshop, you can adjust the default application settings. Most of these options are pretty technical, but we'd like to show you two basic adjustments you may find helpful.

To adjust the default unit:

By default, a document's dimensions are measured in inches. If you're not primarily editing images for prints, we recommend changing this setting to pixels.

Select Edit->Preferences-> Units & Rulers. If you're using a Mac, select Photoshop->Preferences ->Units & Rulers.

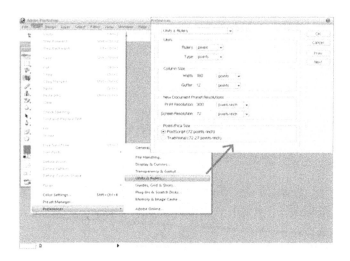

A dialog box will appear. Under Units, click the menu next to Rulers, select Pixels, and click OK. You may need to quit and restart Photoshop for the changes to take effect.

To adjust the text size:

If you'd like the text of the Photoshop interface to be larger or smaller, you can adjust the application's text size.

Select Edit -> Preferences -> Interface (or Photoshop right-arrow Preferences right-arrow Interface on a Mac).

Under Text, click the menu next to UI Font Size, then select the desired size. You may need to quit and restart Photoshop for the changes to take effect.

Changing the zoom level

When you're editing an image in Photoshop, you'll often be viewing it at less than 100% of its full size. That's because most modern digital cameras take large, high-resolution photos. In fact, these images are so large, that most computer screens can't display all of the pixels in the image at once. This is actually a good thing, because it means you'll have extra detail to work with as you edit the image.

If you want to zoom in or out, simply press Ctrl+ or Ctrl- (hold the Ctrl key and then press the + or - key). If you're using a Mac, you'll press Command+ or Command-.

In the example below, you can see a document at 44.4% of its full size. Notice that you can see the current zoom level at the top of the document window, as well as in the bottom-left corner of the screen.

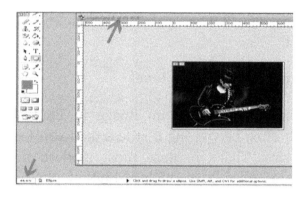

By contrast, the example below shows the same image at 100% (full size). Notice that only part of the image is visible at this zoom level. If desired, you can use the horizontal and vertical scroll bars to view other parts of the image.

To zoom the image to fit the document window, press Ctrl+0 (hold the Ctrl key and then press the zero key). If you're using a Mac, you'll press Command+0. Depending on your computer's graphics card, some zoom levels (such 33.33% and 66.67%) can cause the image to appear pixelated. If this happens, you may want to zoom to 25% or 50% instead.

Lesson 3: The Selection and Retouching Basics

Step 1 of 10:

Use Content-Aware Fill.

Using the lasso tool, select the right-most group of 3 people in the first image at the top. Choose Edit > Fill in the top menu.

Step 2 of 10:

Apply Content-Aware.

Choose Content-Aware in the Use menu and click OK.

Applying Content-Aware, 'Fill' multiple times to the area or part of the area often improves results.

For some images, selecting the Color Adaption check box will provide a smoother color transition. Try it with your photos.

Step 3 of 10:

Use the Content-Aware Move tool.

In the sky image, select the Content-Aware Move Tool (nested under the Spot Healing brush).

In the Options bar, select Move from the Mode menu.

Step 4 of 10:

Reposition the sky streak to the left.

Make a generous selection around the thin streak line with the Content-Aware Move tool (see example).

In the Options bar under Adaptation, enter 5 for the Structure option and 7 for Color.

Drag the streak to the left to see how it blends with its new surroundings.

The Adaptation Options control the blending of the pixels. A higher Structure value (1-7) maintains more of the copied edge pixels. A higher Color value (0-10) provides more color blending.

Step 5 of 10:

Use the Extend Mode.

For the third image (the foliage image), select the Content-Aware Move Tool. In the Options bar, select Extend from the Mode menu.

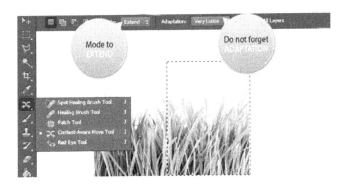

Under Adaption, enter 5 for Structure and 8 for Color. The high Structure level will keep the foliage detailed, and the high level of color will ensure the foliage is well blended in to the existing foliage.

Step 6 of 10:

Make the foliage appear to grow.

Select a portion of the foliage with the tool, like the one in the example to the right. Move your selection to the right, to extend the foliage into the rocky area.

Step 7 of 10:

Use the Spot Healing brush.

In the fourth image, select the Spot Healing brush in the Tools panel.

In the Options bar, set Mode to Replace and Type to Content-Aware.

Step 8 of 10:

Remove the telephone wire using the Spot Healing brush.

Move the brush over one end of the wire. Make sure the brush is larger than the wire. Right-click with your mouse (Control + click on Mac), or use the left [and right] bracket keys to change the brush size to about 64 px.

Click and drag to remove the first portion of the wire. Then repeat to remove the other end of the wire.

Step 9 of 10:

Use the Patch tool.

With the Patch tool, you can choose which area Photoshop uses to fill the area where you remove an object.

Select the Patch tool in the Tool panel (found under the Spot Healing Brush tool). In the Options bar, choose Content-Aware from the Patch Type menu.

Step 10 of 10:

Remove the Banana slug using the Patch tool.

Set Adaptation values. Try Structure = 5, and Color = 4 for this image. The high structure level will keep the rigidity of the tree bark, and a medium color adaption will blend in with the surrounding colors.

With the Patch tool, draw a selection around the slug. Drag your selection to the right of its current position. Release the mouse button and Photoshop heals the area.

Lesson 4: Image Size and Resolution

Photographs and images have found varied usages in the common life; images are required every time you want to fill an application for a job or for a new course. The issue arises when we need to resize the image and keep its resolution intact. Re-sizing is an easy thing but keeping up with the resolution is going to be a task. Here we are going to leverage you with the requisite understanding of the image size and resolution.

Caution: It is of great importance that you are saving the master file with all the layers intact at a different location in your computer. Saving a picture with the original size and resolution leverages you with the opportunity to do a lot of things with the picture and learn new things.

Understanding Resolution: Resolution is the only complicated thing in the world of photography and Photoshop. You will have to develop an intricate understanding of this term to see eye to eye with the photographers and with the clients. The confusion increases by leaps and bounds when you realize that there are two different types of resolution in the world of digital photography.

One of them is Dots per inch and the other one is Pixels per inch. 'Dots per inch' is commonly referred to as 'dpi'; and 'Pixels per inch' is referred to as 'ppi'. 'Pixels per inch' is more prominent and preferred in the contemporary world. Dots per inch is more about printing on paper while Pixel per inch is about digital technologies and manipulation of photos with the help of digital tools, without losing on to the quality of the picture.

Dots per inch (dpi): Dots per inch refers to the potential of an inkjet printer of applying dots over an inch of the paper. Dots per inch when printed with the help of an inkjet printer will also be dependent on the printer for the quality of the picture. The range of dots per inch varies from 720 to 2800 dots. In recent times, the technological developments have increased it up to 3600 dots per inch. The quality of the picture depends on the closeness of the dots. The closer the dots and better the mixing of colors will be and the photo will grow brighter and deeper in sense. The blending of the color is going to affect the tone of the color on the paper.

The quality of paper is also responsible for the resolution of the picture. On a simple white porous paper the setting of 720 dpi works fine while when it comes to glossy paper with smooth texture, settings like 2800 dpi are used for developing a quality output. A higher setting is required because glossy papers are known to soak up the ink faster than normal paper. DPI is used whenever printing is discussed.

Pixels per inch (ppi): Pixel per inch is discussed every time digital photography is mentioned. Unlike the case of dpi, here, digital changes and alteration is discussed instead of printing and type of paper. Pixel per inch is all about the distance of pixels while developing a digital picture. Pixels per inch are an important setting when aiming for high quality output. At times, low setting is desirable while most of the times the setting depends upon the kind of photography the photographer aims to do.

How ppi works: For example, if you have a picture of 122 ppi then the pixels are going to be separated and not overlapped. The final photo must have closer pixels so that the picture looks flawless and smooth.

Tips: A lot of professional photographers are not well versed with terms like ppi and dpi, they generally end up mismatching each other. There are going to be times when they will be using dpi in place of ppi and vice versa. You will have to pay close attention to the image, technology (whether analog or digital) and decide on your own.

Resizing an Image

1. Choose Image> Image Size

2. Use one of the following steps for modifying the preview of the image.

   • Click on the corner of the dialog box and drag it to resize it according to your view.

   • Drag the part of the image you want to view to see the effects of resizing.

   • If you are looking forward to change the magnification, hold ctrl and click on the image for windows user. Mac users can hold command and click on the image.

3. In order to change the unit of measurement for the dimension of pixels, click on the triangle that is present next to the dimensions button and then you can select from the menu.

4. If you are looking forward to maintain the original ratio of the width or height measurement then you will have to check mark on the option of Constrain Proportion.

Checking this option and clicking OK can give you liberty of maintaining original ration.

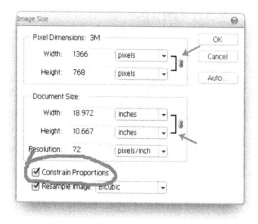

5. You can select one of the following options:

   • If you are planning to change the size or resolution of the image, you will have to see that you are selecting the resample size option available.

   • You will have to select the resample button, if you are planning to change the resolution of the image while changing the size of the image.

   • Or you can go ahead with the resizing of the image without worrying about the resample button.

6. You will now have to ensure that you are entering the values of the width and the height according to your need. In order to enter values, you will have to choose from the menus present next to the width and height text boxes. The new image file size will appear on the top side of the screen. The dialog box will also display the current width and height of the image.

7. For changing the Resolution of the image, you will have to enter the values. You have the liberty of selecting a different unit of measurement. It will help you in understanding the nuances of the product with great ease.

8. If your image has layers and there are styles applied to the layers of the image then you will have to select Scale Style from the gear icon and then scale the effects in the resized image. You can make use of this image only if you had selected Constrain Proportion option.

9. Now that you have changed all the settings according to your need, it is time to do any of the following:

You can change the width, or height of pixels and also that of document sizes.

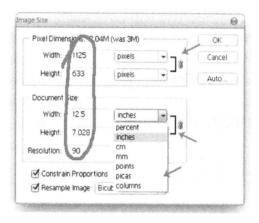

10. Click OK.

Other Resampling Options

Preserve Details: this option will allow you to remove all the noise from the image. The noise reduction options will help you in managing the smoothness of the photo.

Bicubic Smoother: if you are aiming to enlarge the image then this is the best option. The size of the image increases with great ease that too without losing its smoothness.

Bicubic Sharpner: this tool allows you to alter the sharpness of the image. With the efficient use of this tool you will be able to increase the sharpness of the image and make it appear vivid.

Bicubic Smoother: this tool will help you in smoothing the surroundings of the object in the image. You can also make use of complex calculators for managing the smoothness of the image and ensure that a high quality image appears.

Nearest Neighbor: hard edges are going to dilute the quality of your image. You will have to see that you are managing all the edges smoothly and make it look good and better. With this tool you will be able to preserve the hard edges of the image.

Bilinear: this method looks for the surrounding edges of the photos. You can fix the issue with the help of this tool and make your image look prettier and amazingly beautiful.

Creating, opening and importing images from varied sources

There's a lot you can do with your images stored in some decrepitude folder, here are the rest of the amazing options you can depend on and create better images:

Create an Image:

1. Choose file> New

2. Give the new file a name

3. You will have to select the size of the document. You can also specify the type of the document here.

4. Now that you have given it a name, it is time for specifying the height and width of the name.

5. You will also have to select the resizing size of the image and keep it saved in the file.

6. Decide the resolution, color scheme and bit depth and also the color mode of the image.

7. Now that you have placed it on the clipboard, it is going to be occupying a lot of space, so try to complete editing it before moving on to any other image.

8. You will have to select the background scheme of the image and ensure that you are using it properly.

9. Using the preset option select the best image setting for your new image

10. Click ok.

11. Your image is ready. Now you can make use of varied colors, image, graphics and patterns to make your image look really vivid and pretty.

Duplicate an image

There are loads of options. If you simply do not want to create an image then you can go ahead and duplicate an image and make requisite changes into it for making it look prettier and healthier. It is going to benefit your overall color scheme and will make your graphic look really vivid.

1. You will have to select and open the image you want to duplicate.

2. Choose Image> Duplicate. Click on the duplicate button to create a duplicate copy of the image.

3. You will have to enter a new name and save the image according to it.

4. There are loads of options you can make the best use of. There are options like merge layers, select duplicate merged. You will have to preserve the layers of the image with the help of option Deselected.

5. Now that you have done all that is required, it is time for you to click OK and finalize the image.

Open a file using the Open command

1. Choose File> Open

2. Now that you have opened the image, it is time to do all the requisite tasks and make the image of your desire.

3. Click on the open button and start making the image you desire.

4. As soon as you click on the open button, a dialog box will appear and it will provide you with the details of the width, height and the color scheme of the image. You can manipulate the data here to acquire the desired results.

5. You will have to select the name of the article you want to open. If it is not

opening, you will either have to create it or check for it in the other directories.

Note: To specify the number of files listed in the Open Recent menu, change the Recent File List Contains option in the File Handling preferences. Choose Edit > Preferences > File Handling (Windows), or Photoshop > Preferences > File Handling (Mac OS).

Lesson 5: The amazing Photoshop Layers Panel

In Photoshop, layers are utilized to take a shot at individual parts of a picture while not influencing different parts. You may say that layers are similar to straightforwardness. Papers are stacked on top of each other which can be repositioned and independently drawn on without aggravating each other. Each of the things there (comprising of a symbol and a name on a column) is a different layer. One and only one layer can be chosen at once, and all alterations that you make in Photoshop just happen to the layer you are on (unless the change is a conformity layer itself).

Every layer has two cases to one side that show if the layer is unmistakable, chosen, or connected. By tapping on the "eye" symbol, you can conceal the layer. Re-clicking on that case will make the layer unmistakable once more. While tapping on a layer's "eyecon", holding down the "choice" key, will shroud every other layer. Rehashing that stride will make all others obvious once more.

All layers have an aggregate impact upon one another beginning with the layer that is on top. The top layer supersedes all others, and the base ones show through where the top ones aren't obscure. You can change the haziness of every layer by selecting the obscurity in the upper right-hand corner of the palette.

Layers can be moved so one is above another. This rejects the foundation, which is bolted, and can't be moved unless it is reclassified as a layer itself. This is finished by double tapping on it. A standout amongst the most capable functionalities in Photoshop is the ability to overlay pictures and articles on top of one another, and after that change the general haziness of those layers, or specifically change the mistiness in specific ranges of the layer.

Mistiness

Darkness is straight forward. This choice is found in the upper-right-hand corner of the Layers palette. It runs from 0 - 100% mistiness, and is extremely valuable when working with altering shading, sharpness, or whatever other change.

The essential thought is to either duplicate the Background Layer and make any conformity specifically to it (shading changes, honing, blurring, complexity, presentation, and so forth.) or make that modification in an alteration layer.

Once you've made the balanced layer (either utilizing a copied layer or a genuine conformity layer) then Go Overboard!! I mean it... permit yourself to go way sharp, way foggy, way red, way soaked, whatever you're doing, do it more than required.

Layer Masks

How about we discuss layer veil? A layer veil in Photoshop is connected to an individual layer, and is unmistakable in the layers palette as a thumbnail which is connected to the layer's own particular thumbnail. At the point when a layer veil is in this manner connected, its capacity is to tell the Photoshop application how quite a bit of that layer will be unmistakable. On the off chance that the layer veil does not characterize a range as being unmistakable, then it gets to be straightforward.

As you see the veil thumbnail to one side of the layer thumbnail, you will see that it is immaculate white, unadulterated dark, or a two's blend.

Immaculate White = That partition of the layer is 100% Visible

Immaculate Black = That partition is 100% imperceptible.

Now and then you may make segments of the cover a level of dim. This implies that it is not by any means noticeable or straightforward. For this situation the hazy areas essentially have a diminished mistiness in that particular area, much the same as bringing down the general murkiness, yet now it is restricted to that range.

Layer Masks are available in Layers. Picking "Uncover All" makes a white layer cover, and in this manner it uncovers everything. Picking "Shroud All" makes a dark layer veil, and consequently conceals making so as to make everything straightforward.

You might likewise apply a cover speedier by clicking on the Layer Mask symbol in the Layers' base Palette. Essentially tapping on it makes a veil that uncovers all. Choice/Alt - clicking makes a dark veil that conceals all. In the event that you have been utilizing one of the choice instruments, and a layer's segment you are on is chosen, as you make a layer veil, the bit chosen will be white on the cover (uncover all), and the segment not chosen will be dark (shroud all).

You can really paint highly contrasting onto the layer veil (verify it is the cover itself you are painting on), and it will go about as however you seem to be "eradicating" and "painting" the layer now and again. Verify your brush mode is set to "ordinary." You may paint with delicate edge brushes, and brought down obscurity brushes; doing as such will permit you to "quill in" the edges and the layer itself.

All through this instructional exercise, we will be talking about different shading and introduction modification methods. The vast majority of these instruments are accessible as a conformity layer. Most of the picture changes that are accessible at Image/Adjustments are likewise accessible as alteration layers.

Those modifications are effective, however every time you apply them, you are for all time changing the picture's data. For instance, on the off chance that you are "including" Magenta to a picture, you are very smothering the commitment of Green to the picture. (For more information on shading connections perceive how light and shading work).

When that change is made, the old data is gone, and new inserted data is in its stead. In the event that you ever need to return to the first data you will need to insert it back. Addition implies the product program (for this situation Photoshop) scientifically packs or contracts the old data, and chooses what the new values will be.

Whatever alteration you pick will appear as a control panel that you can modify, and once connected it turns into a layer, for example, the highlighted one in the picture below. For this situation, that layer is a bends conformity layer.

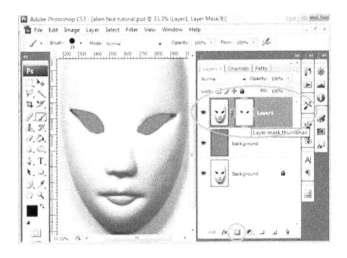

One of the marvels of modification layers is that they "spare" what conformities you have made. Before, you may have taken notes on the acclimation to immersion, or shading adjustment, that achieved a sure result. Never again is that important, the alteration layer does not return back to zeros, it keeps with it with the last data that you connected. You can revive and straighten out any of them whenever, by tapping on the conformity symbol.

You may ask why this theme gets its own segment, that implies you either know everything to blending systems, or you know next to no and don't perceive how effective it can be.

Setting the Background

Opening the foundation is a vital step. The foundation can't be moved unless it is re-imagined as a layer. This is finished by double tapping on it. You can in any case name it foundation on the off chance that you need. However, the default name that Photoshop tries to dole it out is "layer 0".

When the foundation is reclassified as a layer, not just would you be able to set layers beneath it, you can likewise achieve straightforwardness through it. Typically, with a foundation, on the off chance that you eradicate the foundation, or expand the canvas size, what shows through is the foundation shading on the shading palette, whatever that is.

This information may not straightforwardly relate to blending, but rather knowing how to reclassify the foundation will spare some combining migraines.

Converging Down

Frequently you will need to join two layers into one, so that change you make (which isn't layer conformities) will apply to them too. Alert: once layers are converged, there is no doing a reversal!! The two are inseparably associated (at any rate they are difficult to discrete).

On the off chance that you need to have a layer to play around with, and still keep up the first layers, read Merging Visible, beneath. Different explanations behind blending two layers are to set a vector-based thing or a style.

Vector-based things incorporate shapes (lines, circles, and so forth.) attracted Photoshop, and sort. Each of these things is made of vectors, and is just rasterized when you are not taking a shot at its layer. As a vector picture rather than a bitmap, or rasterized picture, a few apparatuses can't be successfully connected to it.

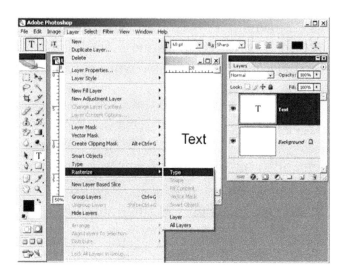

All things considered, you can make another layer (second symbol from the privilege on base of layer palette), which will be straightforward of course. Place it beneath the vector layer and select Merge Down.

Blending Visible

The straightforward Merge Visible does not keep the layer separate that is a propelled strategy I've portrayed underneath this area. Blending noticeable is exactly what it says; every visible layer (those with "eyecons" indicating) is converged into one complete layer, which is presently inseparable.

Blend Visible is found in the same spot as Merge Down. It should be possible through console charges also: order - shift - E for Mac clients, ctrl - shift - E for PC clients. Imperative tip: choice clicking (alt-clicking for PC clients) on any layer's "eyecon" will conceal every single other layer. Rehashing that stride will demonstrate all layers once more. This is helpful when you just need to union a layers' couple, it permits you to shroud the larger part of them rather rapidly.

It additionally helps in perceiving how far you've come in making conformities in the event that you have numerous layers over the foundation picture - you can flip on and off the work's majority you've done.

Blend Visible - Advanced

This is the most ideal approach to blend. You will be making a completely new layer that comprises of the greater part of alternate layers that are noticeable.

You can blend every single obvious layer onto a current layer; however you will then lose the solidarity of that specific layer. Rather, you ought to make another layer, which will be clear and straightforward of course.

With this new layer chosen, and ideally on top of the stack (I'll let you know why in a brief moment), hold down the alternative (alt key for PC clients), while selecting Merge Visible. This duplicates the various layers and consolidations their data onto the new layer.

This layer ought to frequently be on the highest point of the stack, particularly if there are modification layers. This is on the grounds that every single unmistakable layer, including conformity layers is converged into the new layer without being lost. On the off chance that you make this new, combined layer and it wasn't over the conformity layers, but instead dwells underneath them, it will be getting those modifications twice!

Once in light of the fact that the alterations are currently some piece of the new layer, and twice on the grounds that they are under the change layers still! With this new consolidated layer you have the capacity to make changes in accordance with the greater part of the combined layers immediately, or duplicate the layer and have the advantage of replicating all layers together without leveling.

Lesson 6: Blending and Blend Modes

Working with mix modes is quite often an exploratory procedure. Since it's difficult to anticipate the outcomes, you generally appear to wind up exploring different avenues regarding distinctive modes and Fill Opacities until you get the outcomes you're searching for.

In this article I'm going to give you an abnormal state perspective of what the different mix modes do, and afterward I'll dive more profound into the stray pieces of the mix modes by clarifying a math's portion included, and their interrelationships with one another. I'm not going to "demonstrate to" you how the mix modes work—I'm going to "clarify" how they work. When you wrap up this article, you ought to have a superior thought of how to utilize mix modes and where to start your "experimentation," which thusly ought to lessen the time it takes to accomplish the outcomes you're searching for.

How Blend Modes Work

The Opacity slider in the Layers Panel permits you to mix the dynamic layer with the layers beneath by making the dynamic layer translucent, which thus permit the layers underneath to demonstrate through. The mix modes found in Photoshop permit the same procedure to happen, however by utilizing distinctive scientific estimations for every mix mode. As of Photoshop CS5, there are 27 mix modes—2 new mix modes, Subtract and Divide, where as of late included. Any progressions made utilizing mix modes are parametric, i.e., the progressions are non-dangerous, and you can simply return to your mix mode settings and straighten out them as required without harming the pixels in your unique picture.

Shortcuts

The larger part of mix modes have console alternate routes. To utilize these alternate routes, your present instrument must be an option that is other than one of the devices found in the depiction and altering area of the Tools Panel (where the Brush Tool, Healing Brush, Stamp, Eraser, and so on are discovered—see the outline beneath). This is on account of the instruments in the canvas and altering area have mix mode settings they could call their own, and in the event that you have one of these apparatuses chose, their mix mode alternatives will overshadow the mix mode choices found in the Layers Panel. For instance, on the off chance that you utilize Shift+Option+M to change to the Multiply mix mode while you have the Paint apparatus chosen, the Paint instrument's mix mode will be changed to Multiply, not the mix mode choice in the Layers Panel. The uplifting news is that these same mix mode alternate ways DO work for the artistic creation devices; you simply need to pay consideration on what apparatus you have chosen when you utilize the easy routes.

It's likewise conceivable to look up or down the mix mode list by utilizing the console mixes Shift+ (looks down the mix mode rundown), or Shift-(looks up the mix mode list). These console alternate routes likewise work diversely relying upon what apparatus you have chosen in the Tools Panel. For instance, on the off chance that you have the Paint device chosen and you utilize Shift+, the mix mode for the Paint device will look down to the following mix mode in the rundown (not the mix mode in the Layers Panel).

There are likewise console alternate routes for changing the Standard Opacity and Fill Opacity settings in the Layers Panel. To utilize these alternate ways, your present apparatus must be an option that is other than one of the devices found in the work of art and altering area of the Tools Panel. To change the Standard Opacity utilizing the console, simply hit a number. For instance, you can change the mistiness to half by hitting the 5 key, or change the murkiness to 100% by hitting the 0 key. On the off chance that you press the 0 key two times rapidly, you'll change the darkness to 0%. You can even squeeze two distinct numbers in grouping. For instance you can set the obscurity to 35% by squeezing the 3 key immediately took after by the 5 key.

Changing the Fill Opacity works utilizing the same method, yet you have to utilize the Shift key when hitting a number. For instance, to set the Fill Opacity to 33%, utilization the console blends Shift+33. These console alternate ways additionally work when one of the instruments in the artwork and altering area of the Tools Panel is chosen, however by and by; the mix mode settings for these apparatuses outweigh the mix mode settings in the Layers Panel. For instance, on the off chance that you have the Paint apparatus chosen and you utilize the console mix 22, the darkness for the Paint instrument will be changed to 22%. One thing to note is that there isn't a Fill Opacity setting for any of the devices in the artistic creation and altering segment, be that as it may, an instruments' percentage do have a Flow setting (the Brush Tool for instance). For those instruments that have a Flow setting, utilizing Shift+number will change the Flow for the chose apparatus. For instance, in the event that you utilize Shift+22 with the Paint apparatus chosen, the Flow for the Paint instrument will be set to 22.

Each of the mix modes in the Darken gathering has an inverse (integral) mode in the Lighten bunch. These "alternate extremes" utilize marginally distinctive math to touch base at their outcomes, yet the rationale they utilize is comparative yet turned around. For instance, with the Darken mix mode, if the pixels on the dynamic layer are darker than the ones on the layers beneath, they are kept in the picture. The inverse mix mode to Darken is Lighten, and with the Lighten mix mode, if the pixels on the dynamic layer are lighter than the ones on the layers underneath, they are kept in the picture.

The "Exceptional 8" Blend Modes

There are 8 mix modes that I'll be alluding to as the "Exceptional 8." These mix modes carry on diversely when Fill Opacity is balanced, contrasted with when standard Opacity is balanced. The mix modes that aren't individuals from this Special 8 gathering respond the same to both Fill and Opacity changes (accepting there are no Layer Effects), yet with these Special 8 mix modes, 40% Opacity will look not the same as 40% Fill, or 30% Opacity will look not the same as 30% Fill, and so on. For the majority of the other mix modes (the modes that aren't a Special's piece 8), 40% Opacity appears to be identical as 40% Fill, or 20% Opacity has a striking resemblance as 20% Fill, and so forth. This is an imperative idea to comprehend, in light of the fact that it can broaden the abilities of these mix modes. For instance, the Hard mix mode more often than not doesn't look all that incredible, yet when you alter the Fill Opacity for this mode, you can get some awesome results.

Lesson 7: Masks

To understand the concept of Masking in Photoshop and its importance in some areas, we first need to understand what Masking actually means. In simple non-technical terms, Masking seems to be putting a covering over something completely or partially. It is more or less the same in the Photoshop too.

Most of us in the beginning have a fear of the term and think that it is above our understanding limits. I tell you that if you know how to use the Move tool in Photoshop and basic tools then you do not have to panic. It is a concept that uses the simplest things you know and creates a beautiful looking effect that seems to be very tough to create.

In technical terms, Masking is providing transparency in general. You would wonder if opacity would do the same job. It is not actually so. The opacity makes the complete layer transparent or opaque while through masking you can actually provide transparency in certain selected areas. For example, you have two images, which you want to club together and the images have different backgrounds. Then, you can do masking of the images of the areas you want to club.

In all, Masking is the non-destructive method of making certain wanted parts of an image visible over other layered image. It provides the best, most efficient and future oriented approach to editing. It marks the ability and efficiency of a graphic designer.

You may find it not so easy for you to understand it now. This is because this is the first time you are looking towards this. I will advise you to be patient. Because, it is rightly said by a great man 'Everything looks very difficult before it looks easy to you'. When you firstly look at any new thing, it may definitely look confusing to you and this confusion is the test actually. If you leave this here and fail, you may develop an inborn fear in you for the same thing and might never get it. It is always an advice that whenever you start learning a new thing, you should be very patient. Give relevant time to it, no matter you do not get it. With time, you will definitely start grasping and correspondingly you will develop an interest in it. Once you develop an interest in a thing, then you do not need any motivation, you will yourself look for ways to learn it anyhow. Hence, you should always wait for the time to come when you start developing an interest into the subject matter.

I will explain every single step and type of masking in detailed and descriptive manner. After this chapter, you will find yourself completely comfortable with the tool. I guarantee you will be a fan of the tool and always think of editing using the same. You will find different types of images to mask and will realize the designer lust for the tool. A good masking defines good and efficient editing.

Importance of Masking

Masking, for a graphic designer is something like water and oxygen for life. Most of the wedding albums and other edited images follow use of this tool. The tool has several benefits of itself over other methods of creating the same effect. A great graphic designer once said "**Worth doing things in life need layer masks almost all the time**". This shows the love of designers for the tool. The layers were the first thing inculcated into the Photoshop earlier versions, masking came second. Since then, it has developed an impact in the designer's minds.

Masking is used in various fields like-

- You may need masked images for a project in school or college or a presentation. They leave a better impact on the viewer's minds and may fetch you better grades.

- Wedding albums these days have lot many masked images of wedding couples and family members that provide a beautiful impact to the viewer. You can again create masks of images you already have in your collection and give them a new look.

- These images may find their use in Facebook and other social networking site updates. These are very common to see these days. You may find many such updates from people or pages and wonder about their innovation. Now, you can easily understand the sources and it is no more a suspense to you. You can also create some innovative masked images and post on your timeline to make people wonder.

- They may work for some technical purposes, wherein you need to keep fewer pictures and more contents. Here, you mask pictures with contents over each other and use them worthwhile.

Masking is thus a very vital and easy to use tool in Photoshop. It is easy to understand and once you get handy with it, you can find your own new applications for the tool. You can use it for as many purposes as your innovative mind brings you the ideas. It has an unlimited scope of innovation and perfection.

Benefits of Masking over other methods

This is the very first question that clicks a beginner's mind while he reads the definition of Masking. It is an actually good that you come up with such a question. This is because you must have heard of 'You get solutions only if you have questions'. Hence, things will only get clear to you in Photoshop when you think for those, you find relativities among them and try to understand why you chose this particular tool. Otherwise, in an application so bulky and technical like Photoshop, you may need a lot of time to get handy with. And you will still have questions pending unanswered in your mind.

Now, talking about the benefits-

- The first and basic benefit of using masking technique over the opacity method is that in opacity, you will have to use eraser tool to remove the pixels. These pixels are removed from the unwanted areas of the overlying image. Removing of the pixels is never a problem you will say. If in case you need the complete image in future then you will not be able to retain anyhow. This factor makes the opacity reducing method less successful and less feasible than masking.

- Masking provides transparency to the selected certain areas and is a one-step process against the opacity method which involves precision erasing of data. This method is much simpler and easier to apply than others.

- It gives more accuracy and less chances of damage to the original image.

- It consumes much lesser time than any other method and looks attractive to use.

Types of Masking:

Generally, there are two broad categories of Masks. These are –

- Layer masks

- Clipping masks

The two types of masks are closely related in concept, but have many differences in their application. The type of masking you generally get to hear, and the type we have been discussing by now is the Layer Mask. The clipping mask is a much different masking in application. We will discuss about these masking techniques in detail further. Before that, you shall understand the basic difference between the two.

In layer mask, if you want the entire layer to be at 30%, you would lower the opacity, if you want just the left side of a layer to be at 30%, you would use a mask.

When you add the mask to any layer, it shall cover the entire thing with an invisible looking greyscale canvas. There are ways to see it that we will check out later but just keep in mind that like a general rule, applying a mask to a layer won't cause any immediate visual differences unless you have an active selection at the time.

On this invisible canvas, you can paint White, Black or any level of Grey in-between. The color that you paint tells Photoshop how opaque to make the pixels at that point. White means 100% opacity and black means 0% opacity.

Although, **clipping masks** are very similar to layer masks. The only difference is that you use one layer to determine the transparency of another in the layer mask. In this scenario, you stack two layers on top of each other with the bottom being the determining factor of the transparency of the top.

Instead of using values of black and white, though, clipping mask borrows transparency from the layers simply used to make them, namely the bottom layer. If the bottom layer has some areas, that are opaque and some areas that are transparent, a clipping mask will apply these values to the top layer.

Features of masking of a Layer:

There are several features or say proceedings which you need to understand before going through the actual procedure. This is like making a complete knowledge of the weapons before landing into a war situation. If you are unaware of the weapons or their use, you may lose your life or may threat someone else's. Similarly, here you must first get handy with the operations of masking the layers and then whenever you need to perform any of the operation, you will not have to think or find your notes for looking the procedure of the operation you thought to perform. With the perfection of the small things comes the excellence in editing and designing features. Given and explained below are some of the operations, which form the basis of masking or say Layer mask. It is advised to practice all of them independently one after the other for some time, so that when you are following the procedure of masking you do not hesitate in between and fluently go with the flow. This will resist you from irritation and bring perfection in you easily.

How to add a Mask layer that Hides / Shows the Entire Layer

1. Choose- Deselect from the Select Menu and you can clear any selection borders in the image.

2. In the Layers Palette, select the layer or set of layers to which you want to add a mask.

3. Opt one of the following options ahead-

   a) For creating an entire layer-revealing mask, click on the New Layer Mask button in the Layers Palette, or you can choose Add Layer Mask -> Reveal All from the Layer Menu.

   b) For creating an entire layer-hiding mask, Alt plus click (win) or Option-click (Mac) on the

New Layer Mask button or choose Add Layer Mask -> Hide All from the Layer Menu.

How to opt for Editing of a Layer Mask:

1. Click on the layer mask thumbnail in the Layers Palette for making it active.

2. Then you can select any of the editing or say painting tools as per choice.

   Keep in mind, the background and foreground colors are default to gray scale values in the case of active mask.

3. Opt for one of the following options-

   a) For subtracting from the mask and revealing the layer, you can paint the mask with white color.

   b) For making the layer partially visible, you can paint the mask with grey tones of color.

   c) For adding to the mask and hide the layer or set of layers, you can paint the mask with black color. For editing the layer instead of the layer mask, you may select it by clicking its thumbnail in the Layers Palette. The paintbrush icon appears on the left of the thumbnail for indicating that you are editing the layer.

How to add a Mask layer that Hides/Shows a Selection:

1. In the Palette (layers), do select the layer or set of layers to which you want to add the mask.

2. Then, select the desired area in the image, and opt for one of the following options:

   a. Click on the New Layer Mask button in the Layers Palette for creating a mask layer that reveals the selection.

   b. Choose Add Layer Mask -> Reveal Selection option or Hide Selection option from the Layer Menu you see in front of you.

How to go for Selecting and Displaying the Layer Mask:

- Press Alt + click (in windows) or Option-click (in Mac) on the layer mask thumbnail in the Layers Palette for selecting and displaying only the gray scale mask channel. The 'eye icon' in the Layers Palette is dim because all layers or the set of layers are not visible. For redisplaying all the layers, Alt + click or Option click the layer mask thumbnail, or click on the eye icon.

- Hold down Alt + Shift (in win) or Option + Shift (in Mac), and click on the layer mask thumbnail to view the mask on the top of the layer in a 'Rubylith' masking color. Hold down Alt + Shift or Option + Shift and click on the thumbnail again to turn off the color display.

How To Enable or Disable a Layer Mask:

- Shift + click on the Layer Mask thumbnail in the Layers Palette.

- Select the Layer, one with the Layer Mask you want to disable or enable, and choose Disable

Layer Mask or Enable Layer Mask from the Layer Menu.

- A red X appears over the mask thumbnail in the Layers Palette when the mask is disabled and the layer's content appears without the masking effects.

Applying and Discarding of the Masks of layers:

When you finish creating of a Layer Mask, you can either apply the mask layer and make the changes permanent or discard the mask without applying changes. Because Layer Masks are stored as alpha channels, applying and discarding Layer masks can help reduce file size.

1. Click the Layer Mask thumbnail in the Layers Palette.

2. To remove the Layer Mask by making changes permanent, click on the Trash button at the bottom of the Layers Palette, and then click Apply.

3. To remove the Layer Mask without applying the changes, click on the Trash button at the

bottom of the Layers Palette, and then click Discard.

Unlinking of Layers and Masks:

- In default, a layer or set of layers is linked to its layer mask or say vector mask, as indicated by the link icon between the thumbnails in the Layers Palette.

- The layer and its mask move all together in the image when you move either one of them with the Move tool. Unlinking of the layers lets you move them independently and shift the mask's boundaries separately from the layer.

- Click on the link icon in the Layer Palette for unlinking a layer from its mask.

- Click between the layer and mask path thumbnails in the Layers Palette to re-establish the link between a layer and its mask.

How to load a Layer or Boundaries of a Mask as a Selection:

By loading a Mask of a layer, you can quickly select all the opaque areas on the layer -- that is, the areas within the boundaries of the layer. This is useful when you want to exclude transparent areas from any selection. You can also load the boundaries of a Layer mask as a selection.

a) In the Layers Palette, press Ctrl + click (in win) or Command-click (in Mac) on the Layer or Layer Mask thumbnail.

b) For adding the pixels to an existing selection, press Ctrl + Shift (in win) or press Command + Shift (in Mac), and click on the Layer or Layer Mask thumbnail in the Layers Palette.

c) For subtracting the pixels from an existing selection, press Ctrl + Alt (in win) or press Command + Option (in Mac), and click on the Layer or Layer Mask thumbnail in the Layers Palette.

d) For loading the intersection of the pixels and an existing selection, press Ctrl + Alt + Shift (in win) or press Command + Option + Shift (in

Mac), and click on the layer or the layer mask thumbnail in the layer palette.

Know the types of the Masks:

Masks are divided under two broad categories. These categories are as follows –

- Layer Masks- First category is the layer masks. We have been talking about them since the start. Layer masks are bitmap images that are dependent on the resolution. Their creation is possible with the selection or the painting tools in general.

- Vector Masks- Second broad category is Vector masks. These are dependent on the resolution, but their creation is possible with the pen or shape tools.

  NOTE: The way of creation is the basic difference between the two categories of masks.

Quick mask mode:

This mode is a special feature of masking. It lets you make any editing to the selection as a mask. The biggest advantageous factor with editing your selection as a mask is that you can use any Photoshop tool or filter for modifying the mask almost. For example, you create a rectangular selection with the Marquee tool available, you can enter the Quick Mask Mode and use the paintbrush to extend or to contract the selection process, or you can use a filter to distort the edges of the selection. You can also use selection tools available, because the quick mask is not a selection.

How to Use a Quick Mask Mode:

It is equally important for you to know how to use the feature as to know the use of it. For using the Quick Mask Mode, you can start with a selection and then 'add to' or 'subtract from' it for making the mask. Alternately, you may create the mask entirely in Quick Mask mode. Color differentiates the protected and the unprotected areas of selection. When you leave Quick Mask Mode, the unprotected areas become a selection.

A temporary channel of Quick Mask appears in the Channels Palette while you are working in the Quick Mask mode. However, you perform the entire mask editing job in the image window.

- By using any selection tool, you should select the part of the image you want to change.

- Click on the Quick Mask Mode button in the toolbox. A 'color overlay' covers and protects the area outside the selection. Selected areas are left unprotected by this mask. By default, Quick Mask Mode colors the protected area using a red 50% opaque overlay.

- For editing the mask, you should select a painting tool from the toolbox. The swatches in the toolbox automatically become black and white.

- Color with white to select more of an image (the color overlay is removed from areas painted with white).

- To deselect areas, paint over them with black color (the color overlay covers areas painted with black).

- Painting with grey or any other color creates a semi-transparent area, useful for feathering or anti-aliased effects (semi-transparent areas may not appear selected when you exit Quick Mask Mode, but they are)

- Click on the Standard Mode button in the toolbox to turn off the Quick Mask Mode and return to your original image. A selection border now surrounds the unprotected area of the quick mask. If a feathered mask is converted to a selection, the boundary line runs halfway between the black pixels and the white pixels of the mask gradient.

- The boundary of selection indicates the pixels transition from being less than fifty percent selected to more than fifty percent selected area.

- Apply the changes you desire to the image affected but only in the selected area.

- From the options, choose Deselect from the Select Menu to deselect the selection, or the option Save Selection from the Select Menu to save the selection.

Hence, after this you can practice using this special feature of masking called Quick mask Mode as it has its own importance in some areas. Read the procedure twice or thrice and then only start practicing or you shall irritate yourself up.

With this, you now need to know the new term that comes. This is 'Alpha Channels'. Now follows the details on the alpha channels. I will explain what they are, how are they useful to you, how do they relate to the masking concept, and how you can use them.

ALPHA channels

These are the channels, which allow you to save and load selections. You can do editing of the Alpha channels using any of the editing tools available. When you choose a channel out of the many, in the Channels palette, foreground and background colors appear as greyscale values.

How to Store Masks in an Alpha Channel:

Now follows the main use of alpha channels in masking and you shall get your answer for studying this feature. In addition to temporary Masks available in Quick Mask Mode, you can create many permanent masks. This is possible by storing these masks in alpha channels.

This allows you and helps you in using the masks again in the same image or in a different image. You can create an alpha channel in and then add a mask to it. You can also save an existing selection in an image as an alpha channel that will appear in the Channels Palette.

How to create Alpha Channels:

Here follows the procedure of creating these alpha channels. Go through the step wise procedure carefully and try to understand the steps so that you may use this for ease.

- Click on the New Channel button at the bottom of the Channels Palette.

- Use a painting or editing tool to paint in the image. Paint with black to add to the channel; paint with white to remove from the channel.

- Click the 'eye icon' next to a color (or composite) channel for displaying the image with a color overlay.

How to Save a Mask Selection:

- Do select the area or areas of the image you are working on, that you want to isolate.

- Click the 'Save Selection' button at the bottom of the Channels Palette.

- A new channel appears, named according to the sequence by which it was created.

How to load a Selection into an Image:

- Select the alpha-channel.

- Click on the Load Selection button at the bottom of the Palette.

- Then click on the composite color channel.

Procedures and different methods of masking:

Finally, now you are ready to go through the procedural steps of the masking technique. In case, I would have directly brought you to the procedure, most chances are that you would have not got anything or may not excel as good as you would now after getting handy with all the operations taught above.

I will frame the procedural steps now based on different masking and explain it briefly to you. It will follow the layer mask, clipping mask and all other small possibilities in which you may have problem.

Let us start with the Black and White Layer Masks.

Black and White Layer Masks:

- This is what we call the Layer Mask. Here, when you make a click on the Layer Mask button in the Layers palette, Photoshop adds a white layer mask, which reveals the entire image.

- To start with a white layer mask is a subtractive mode of working. Here, you see the entire image and paint away with the black or grey areas you do not want to see in your image.

- Press Option + clicking (in Mac) or press Alt-clicking (in windows), the Layer Mask button adds a black layer mask, which hides the entire layer.

- Now you need to paint with white color to add the image back—to work additively you bring the image back into view.

Use:

The technique described above, is generally, used to retouch portraits by photographers. Photographers do sharpen the entire portrait, and then they add a black layer mask to the sharpened layer. Then they paint back in the sharpness and where ever it is required — in most cases the eyes and lips of the person.

Clipping Mask (When you take two different layers and choose one as background):

- You can open both the images you want to mask and decide which one will serve as the image background and which will overlay.

- Use the Move tool to drag the overlying one over to the background image and name the layer as per your choice.

- Now, Click on the Layer Mask button.

- Note that nothing has changed in your image and that Photoshop has added a white layer mask to the overlying image

- Paint with a soft black colored brush over those areas of the overlying layer that you do not want to see.

- If accidently, you paint over an area that you do want to see, you can press 'X' to switch the foreground and background colors, and paint over the area you want to see with white.

- Keep in your mind, 'white reveals and black conceals'—meaning that if you paint with black on the layer mask, you will be hiding "overlying layer" pixels.

- Painting with a large and soft black colored brush quickly conceals the areas of the overlying image you do not want to see anymore.

- The Power of Layer Masking - Adding a white layer mask does not alter the image in any way.

- In a few minutes, you should have the image roughly combined. To fine-tune the image edges, zoom in on an area and paint with a smaller and a harder brush.

- Press "X" to paint with black or conceal, or white to reveal the overlying layer.

- Press Option + click or Alt + click accordingly on the layer mask to view it.

- When you have finished it, select File -> Save As and save the file in the PSD or TIFF format. These are the two recommended formats maintaining the layers.

- When you return to this image, you can readjust it any way you want by painting on the layer mask again.

After reading this procedure, you actually know the steps for masking an image over the other. For perfection in work, you will have to spend many evenings practicing different types of images. Now for innovation or say creating something outstanding, it is always your mind or the ideas. The technique remains the same.

Different types of Layer Masks:

Now understand the different types of layer masks in detail that will help you understand better.

Feature- Knowing Gradated Layer Masks:

The largest paintbrush in Adobe Photoshop is the Gradient tool. You can use it on layer masks to control the tonal and the color effects and to blend the images together seamlessly.

Feature- How and why to Darken Image Edges

Why to choose edges darkening procedure-

- The adjustment Layers available in combination with the blending modes and layer masks offer a straightforward method for lightening and darkening the areas in an image where you want to draw public attention. Light areas attract the viewer's focus, whereas dark areas are of less visual interest.

- Traditionally, photographers used to burn or darken the edges of their prints to focus the viewer's attention on the centre. If you employ this technique, you should do it as subtly as possible so that it is not noticeable.

- After finishing a composite completely, I often add a slight edge burn to darken the outer edges and keep the viewer's eyes focused on the centre.

You can quickly create this darkening effect using following steps-

- An Adjustment Layer and the Gradient tool are the basic needs.

- Activate the topmost layer of your composite or image.

- Add a Level or Curve Adjustment Layer— it does not matter which one you choose. As soon as the interface pops up, click OK without changing anything.

- Change the blending mode to 'Multiply' and reduce the opacity to 50 percent. The entire image will become darker.

- Select Image -> Adjustments -> Invert or press Command + I or Ctrl + I to invert the layer mask, which will turn it blackish.

- Activate the Gradient tool and select the second gradient from the Gradient picker— Foreground to Transparent.

- Press 'f' to place the image into full-screen mode and zoom out to see the entire image. I prefer to start the gradient well outside the image. Pull first gradient from the upper left toward the centre of the image, and then repeat on all four corners.

- Turn the Image Adjustment Layer view column on and off to view the image with and without the darkening effect. If you like what you see, save the file. If you are not satisfied, maybe it is too light or too dark; do adjust the layer opacity to create the desired effect.

Feature-How to Balance an Image Exposure:

Using the Gradient tool on a Levels or Curves Adjustment Layer is a quick and easy method for balancing exposure.

To balance the image exposure, you may use a Curves Adjustment Layer with a gradated mask as follows:

- After scanning the image, you can add a Curves Adjustment Layer and lightened the entire image

- By using a black-to-white gradient from right to left, you can conceal the tonal change on the correct side of the image and let the change show through on the left, which lightened the left side and balance the exposure perfectly.

- The Gradient tool conceals the change on one side of the image and reveals it on the other side.

Feature-How to adjust Position:

The layer and the layer mask are adjusted together or independently over one another. To move the layer and mask together, make sure they are linked to each other. To move either one independently, you have to unlink them by clicking on a small chain between the layer and the Layer Mask icon.

Feature-How to Blend Images seamlessly:

To build image backgrounds by combining two or more images is a fantastic method of building up a pile of creative backdrops. The Gradient tool can help you achieve good results very quickly. The steps follow-

- Open the two images you want to blend and then determine - which one will serve as the background and which one will be in the foreground.

- Drag the top image over to the bottom image with the Move tool. Drag quickly and with confidence. Pressing and holding the Shift key will place the top image exactly on the centre point of the bottom image.

- Add a layer mask to the top image and reduce the layer opacity to 50 percent. This helps you find the best position for the image.

- Click on the layer mask to make sure it is active, activate the Gradient tool, and choose the third gradient from the gradient library— black to white.

- Start the gradient where you want the bottom image to show through completely and draw up. Release the mouse when you reach the point in the top image that you want to see completely

- Increase the layer opacity to 100 percent again to see the results.

- After dragging one image onto another, reduce the layer opacity so that you can view the relationship between the two.

- Use a black-to-white gradient to reveal the buildings in the lower part of the image.

- Set layer opacity to 100 percent to see the image combination.

Feature- What is experimentation in masking?

The best thing about Gradient tool and layer mask is that you can redo the blend over and again to get the image exactly right.

Take a moment to experiment with the Gradient tool—create very steep transitions by only drawing for a short distance

Create a very long transition by drawing the gradient across the entire image.

Try it going from right to left, or diagonally. Every time you draw a new gradient, the previous blend is overwritten, which, lets you experiment to your heart's content.

Feature - How to refine blended Images?

Many a times an image combination requires more than a straight-line gradient to blend in a new background. Combine the Gradient and Brush tools to refine layer masks to improve images. Steps are as follows-

- You can start with opening both the images and drag the overlying image on top of the background image.

- Now, add a layer mask to the overlying image and draw a gradient from below the horizon to the top of the new overlying image. Now the problem is that the new overlying image is covering the background, which of course needs to be in front of the overlying image.

- The initial gradient on layer mask adds the overly but covers the background.

- Click on the sky layer mask, and using a black brush with 50 percent hardness, carefully paint inside the pony to block the sky from being visible.

- Press Option + click or Alt + click on the layer mask to see exactly what is going on—the gradient is letting the new overlying image blend in, and the black areas are blocking the overly from affecting the background.

- If by chance, you paint into the overly overlying, Press Option + click or Alt + click to check for the gradient directly adjacent to the mistake. This samples the grey with the density of the gradient, and as you paint the overly will blend in without showing any density differences.

- Painting on the layer mask protects the background from being affected by the sky layer.

- If necessary, Press Option + click or Alt + click to sample darker or lighter density areas from the gradient as you work up or down the pony's head.

Feature- Get to know the Selective Changes:

While you make a selection and add an Adjustment Layer, Adobe Photoshop automatically transfers active selection to the layer mask and the adjustments only take place within the active areas themselves.

Steps are as follows-

- You can select the sign with the Polygon Lasso tool and feather the selection by 1 pixel to soften the edges ever so slightly.

- Then add a Curves Adjustment Layer and raise the mid-tones.

- As you can see, Photoshop has already transferred the Lasso selection into the layer mask. The selected area—the sign—is white, so the Curves correction only takes place through the white areas of the mask, lightening the dark sign.

- Now, select the area you need to change.

Feature - How to merge Photographic Exposure

Most photographers always look for better tools and techniques to express their vision. They not always allow the limitations of their tools negatively create impact on the quality of the final image.

- Some of the limitations photographers have to face include:

- The dynamic range of the scene is wider than the digital camera or film can capture.

- The lens is not wide enough to frame the full grandeur of the scene.

- The natural light does not illuminate the scene properly.

- The scene contains mixed color temperatures that conflict with one another.

- Today, most photographers still face these challenges, but their tools have improved a bit—they use professional digital cameras and can preview their images on their laptops while on location or on their set.

The biggest advantage of working with a professional digital camera is that a photographer can combine a series of exposures or acquire the file with multiple settings in Photoshop to achieve the following:

- Extend the dynamic range.

- Expand the view of the scene.

- Capture light over time.

- Color and balance a scene when you do not need to gel or to filter the lights or lens.

Feature- How to Increase the Dynamic Range:

Any consummate professional photographer— skilled, talented, creative, conscientious, and always ready to try new tools and techniques to produce better images, imagine having worked for over 20 years with film technology, is now an avowed digital photographer taking great pleasure in planning, composing, and compositing images.

One of his specialties is interior and exterior architectural photography—a field that brings many constraints and challenges with it.

For example, it is tough to move a building to face the light, or to close the window to control the exposure, when the client wants to see the beautiful view and the interior of the room simultaneously.

He photographs with high-end, digital cameras. After framing the image, he locks down his camera on the tripod and takes separate exposures for shadows, mid-tones, and highlights to create images that hold information from the darkest shadows to the brightest highlights.

Summary:

After thoroughly going through all the points, you come to know about every big and small concept and operation involved in the masking process. After this, it is all about the practice and innovation that defines your excellence. Stay in touch with the concept or you may lose it anytime.

Lesson 8: Working with the camera raw plug-in

Basic concept:

The Camera Raw adds functionality to the Adobe Bridge. The camera raw installs as a plug-in. It is the method for processing raw digital captures into standard RGB files, and it does so with enormous power and flexibility. Camera Raw presents the multi-tabbed interface with lots and lots of sliders and pop-up menus. It is very vital to use each adjustment and menu very correctly and efficiently. With a little practice, it can become a second thought for you, and you can be quick to get the exact global color and the tone corrections for your raw captures. However, the 'Camera Raw' really only makes global corrections—to go further with your image adjustments on a local basis, you'll need to follow up in Photoshop.

Now, I will deliver the complete details of the Camera-Raw plug in feature step-by-step. Go through the steps closely and follow the set of instructions simultaneously. This is the best possible way of going through this topic. All the specific operations, the uses and required knowledge are being imparted ahead.

How to make color and the tonal adjustments in Camera Raw:

The color and tonal adjustments is a special feature:

Get to see how to preview highlight and shadow clipping:

The clipping occurs when the various color values of a pixel are higher than the highest value or lower than the lowest value that can be represented in the image. Over bright values are clipped to output white, and over dark values are clipped to output black. The result is the loss of image detail.

- For seeing which pixels are being clipped with the rest of the preview image, select Shadows or Highlights options at the top of the histogram. Or you may press U to see shadow clipping, O to see highlight clipping.

- For seeing only the pixels that are being clipped, press Alt (in windows) or Option (in Mac OS) while dragging the Exposure, Recovery, or Blacks sliders.

For the Exposure and Recovery sliders, the image turns black, and clipped areas appear white. For the Blacks slider, the image turns white and clipped areas appear black. Colored areas indicate clipping in one color channel (red, green, blue) or two color channels (cyan, magenta, yellow).

Note that, in some cases, clipping occurs because the color space that you are working in has a gamut that is too small. If your colors are being clipped, consider working in a color space with a large gamut, such as 'ProPhoto' RGB.

Understanding the White balance controls:

For adjusting the white balance, you need to identify which objects in the image you want to be neutral-colored (white or grey), and then have to adjust the colors to make those objects neutral. A white or grey object in a scene takes on the color cast by the ambient light or flash used to shoot the picture. When you use the White Balance tool to specify an object that you want white or grey, Camera Raw can determine the color of the light in which the scene was shot and then adjust for scene lighting automatically. Color temperature (in Kelvin) is used as a measure of scene lighting. Natural and incandescent light sources give off light in a predictable distribution according to their temperature.

A digital camera records the white balance at the time of exposure as a metadata entry. The Camera Raw plug-in reads this value and makes it the initial setting when you open the file in the Camera Raw dialog box. This setting, usually yields the correct color temperature, or nearly so. You can adjust the white balance if it is not right.

Note that, not all color casts are a result of incorrect white balance. Use the DNG Profile Editor to correct a color cast that remains after the white balance is adjusted. See Adjust color rendering for your camera in Camera Raw. The Basic tab in the Camera Raw dialog box has three controls for correcting a color cast in an image:

White Balance Camera Raw applies the white balance setting and changes the Temperature and Tint properties in the Basic tab accordingly. Use these controls to fine-tune the color balance.

As Shot Uses the camera's white balance settings, if they are available.

Auto Calculates the white balance based on the image data.

Camera raw and DNG files also have the following white balance settings: Daylight, Cloudy, Shade, Tungsten, Fluorescent, and Flash.

Note that, If Camera Raw doesn't recognize the white balance setting of a camera, choosing As Shot is the same as choosing Auto.

Temperature sets the white balance to a custom color temperature. Decrease Temperature to correct a photo taken with a lower color temperature of light; the Camera Raw plug-in makes the image colors bluer to compensate for the lower color temperature (yellowish) of the ambient light. Conversely, increase Temperature to correct a photo taken with a higher color temperature of light; the image colors become warmer (yellowish) to compensate for the higher color temperature (bluish) of the ambient light.

Note that, the range and units for the Temperature and Tint controls are different when you are adjusting a TIFF or JPEG image. For example, Camera Raw provides a true-temperature adjustment slider for raw files from 2,000 Kelvin to 50,000 Kelvin. For JPEG or TIFF files, Camera Raw attempts to approximate a different color temperature or white balance. Because the original value was already used to alter the pixel data in the file, Camera Raw does not provide the true Kelvin temperature scale. In these instances, an approximate scale of -100 to 100 is used in place of the temperature scale.

Tint- Sets the white balance to compensate for a green or magenta tint. Decrease Tint to add green to the image; increase Tint to add magenta.

To adjust the white balance quickly, select the White Balance tool and then click an area in the image that you want to be a neutral grey. The Temperature and Tint properties adjust to make the selected color exactly neutral (if possible). If you're clicking whites, choose a highlight area that contains significant white detail rather than a specular highlight. You can double-click the White Balance tool to reset White Balance to As Shot.

Understanding the Histogram and RGB levels:

Histogram is nothing but a representation of number of pixels at each luminance value in an image. A histogram that has non-zero values for each luminance value indicates an image that takes advantage of the full tonal scale. A histogram that does not use the full tonal range corresponds to a dull image that lacks contrast. A histogram with a spike at the left side indicates shadow clipping; a histogram with a spike on the right side indicates highlight clipping.

One common task for adjusting an image is to spread out the pixel values more evenly from left to right on the histogram, instead of having them bunched up at one end or the other.

A histogram is made up of three layers of color that represent the red, green, and blue color channels. White appears when all three channels overlap. Yellow, magenta, and cyan appear when two of the RGB channels overlap (yellow equals the red + green channels, magenta equals the red + blue channels, and cyan equals the green + blue channels).

The histogram changes automatically as you adjust the settings in the Camera Raw dialog box.

The RGB values of the pixel under the pointer (in the preview image) appear below the histogram.

Note that, you can also use the Color Sampler tool to place up to nine color samplers in the preview image. The RGB values appear above the preview image. To remove a color sampler, press Alt-click in windows or Option + click in Mac OS. To clear the color samplers, click Clear Samplers.

The Camera Raw dialog box displays the RGB values of the pixel under the pointer.

How to fine-tune tone of the curves:

Use the controls in the Tone Curve tab to fine-tune images after you have made tone adjustments in the Basic tab. The tone curves represent changes made to the tonal scale of an image. The horizontal axis represents the original tone values of the image (input values), with black on the left and progressively lighter values toward the right. The vertical axis represents the changed tone values (output values), with black on the bottom and progressing to white at the top.

If a point on the curve moves up, the output is a lighter tone; if it moves down, the output is a darker tone. A straight, 45-degree line indicates no changes to the tone response curve: the original input values exactly match the output values.

Use the tone curve in the nested Parametric tab to adjust the values in specific tonal ranges in the image. The areas of the curve affected by the region properties (Highlights, Lights, Darks, or Shadows) depend on where you set the split controls at the bottom of the graph. The middle region properties (Darks and Lights) mostly affect the middle region of the curve. The Highlight and Shadows properties mostly affect the ends of the tonal range.

To adjust tone curves, do any of the following:

- To Drag the Highlights, Lights, Darks, or Shadows slider in the nested Parametric tab. You can expand or contract the curve regions that the sliders affect by dragging the region divider controls along the horizontal axis of the graph.

- To drag a point on the curve in the nested Point tab. As you drag the point, the Input and Output tonal values are displayed beneath the tone curve.

- For this, choose an option from the Curve menu in the nested Point tab. The setting you choose is reflected in the Point tab, but not in the settings in the Parametric tab. Medium Contrast is the default setting.

- Do Select the Parametric Curve Targeted Adjustment tool in the toolbar and drag in the image. The Parametric Curve Targeted Adjustment tool adjusts the Highlights, Lights, Darks, or Shadows curve region based on the values in the image where you click.

Note that, Targeted Adjustment tool does not affect point curves.

What is Clarity, Vibrance, and Saturation controls?

You can modify the color saturation of all the colors by adjusting the Clarity, Vibrance, and Saturation controls on the Basic tab. (To adjust saturation for a specific range of colors, use the controls on the HSL / Greyscale tab.)

Clarity– Makes an addition to depth of an image by increasing local contrast, with greatest effect on the mid-tones. This setting is like a large-radius un-sharp mask. When using this setting, it is best to zoom in to 100% or greater. For maximizing the effect, increase the setting until you see halos near the edge details of the image and then reduce the setting slightly.

Vibrance- Adjusts the saturation so that clipping is minimized as colors approach full saturation. This setting changes the saturation of all lower-saturated colors with less effect on the higher-saturated colors. Vibrance also prevents skin tones from becoming oversaturated.

Saturation- Adjusts the saturation of all image colors equally from -100 (monochrome) to +100 (double the saturation).

How to adjust the tone:

You adjust the image tonal scale using the tone controls in the Basic tab.

When you click Auto at the top of the tone controls section of the Basic tab, Camera Raw analyzes the image and makes automatic adjustments to the tone controls.

You can also apply automatic settings separately for individual tone controls. To apply an automatic adjustment to an individual tone control, such as Exposure or Contrast, press Shift and double-click the slider. To return an individual tone control to its original value, double-click its slider.

When you adjust tone automatically, Camera Raw ignores any adjustments previously made in other tabs (such as fine tuning of tone in the Tone Curves tab). For this reason, apply automatic tone adjustments first—if at all—to get an initial approximation of the best settings for your image. If you are careful during shooting and have deliberately shot with different exposures, you probably don't want to undo that work by applying automatic tone adjustments. On the other hand, you can always try clicking Auto and then undo the adjustments if you don't like them.

Previews in Adobe Bridge use the default image settings. If you want the default image settings to include automatic tone adjustments, select Apply Auto Tone Adjustments in the Default Image settings section of the Camera Raw preferences.

Note that, if you are comparing images based on their previews in Adobe Bridge, leave the Apply Auto Tone Adjustments preference deselected, which is the default. Otherwise, you'll be comparing images that have already been adjusted. As you make adjustments, keep an eye on the end points of the histogram, or use the shadow and highlight clipping previews.

While moving the tone controls sliders, hold down Alt (in windows) or Option (in Mac OS) to preview where highlights or shadows are clipped. Move the slider until clipping begins, and then reverse the adjustment slightly. (For more information, see Preview highlight and shadow clipping in Camera Raw.)

• To manually adjust a tone control, drag the slider, type a number in the box, or select the value in the box and press the Up or Down arrow key.

• To reset a value to its default, double-click the slider control.

Note that, the tone controls that appear in the Basic panel depend on whether you are working in Process Version PV2012, PV2010, or PV2003, as noted.

Exposure (All): Adjusts the overall image brightness. Adjust the slider until the photo looks good and the image is the desired brightness. Exposure values are in increments equivalent to aperture values (f-stops) on a camera. An adjustment of +1.00 is similar to opening the aperture 1 stop. Similarly, an adjustment of -1.00 is like closing the aperture 1 stop.

Contrast (All): Increases or decreases image contrast, mainly affecting mid tones. When you increase contrast, the middle-to-dark image areas become darker, and the middle-to-light image areas become lighter. The image tones are inversely affected as you decrease contrast.

Highlights (PV2012): Adjusts bright image areas. Drag to the left to darken highlights and recover "blown out" highlight details. Drag to the right to brighten highlights while minimizing clipping.

Shadows (PV2012): Adjusts dark image areas. Drag to the left to darken shadows while minimizing clipping. Drag to the right to brighten shadows and recover shadow details.

Whites (PV2012): Adjusts white clipping. Drag to the left to reduce clipping in highlights. Drag to the right to increase highlight clipping. (Increased clipping may be desirable for specular highlights, such as metallic surfaces.)

Blacks (PV2012): Adjusts black clipping. Drag to the left to increase black clipping (map more shadows to pure black). Drag to the right to reduce shadow clipping.

Blacks (PV2010 and PV2003): Specifies which image values map to black. Moving the slider to the right increases the areas that become black, sometimes creating the impression of increased image contrast. The greatest effect is in the shadows, with much less change in the mid-tones and highlights.

Recovery (PV2010 and PV2003): Attempts to recover details from highlights. Camera Raw can reconstruct some details from areas in which one or two color channels are clipped to white.

Fill Light (PV2010 and PV2003): Attempts to recover details from shadows, without brightening blacks. Camera Raw can reconstruct some details from areas in which one or two color channels are clipped to black. Using Fill Light is like using the shadows portion of the Photoshop® Shadow/Highlight filter or the After Effects® Shadow/Highlight effect.

Brightness (PV2010 and PV2003): Adjusts the brightness or darkness of the image, much as the Exposure property does. However, instead of clipping the image in the highlights or shadows, Brightness compresses the highlights and expands the shadows when you move the slider to the right. Often, the best way to use this control is to set the overall tonal scale by first setting Exposure, Recovery, and Blacks; then set Brightness. Large Brightness adjustments can affect shadow or highlight clipping, so you may want to readjust the

Exposure, Recovery, or Blacks property after adjusting

What are HSL / Greyscale controls?

You can use the controls in the HSL / Greyscale tab to adjust individual color ranges. For example, if a red object looks too vivid and distracting, you can decrease the Reds values in the nested Saturation tab.

The following nested tabs contain controls for adjusting a color component for a specific color range:

Hue Changes the color. For example, you can change a blue sky (and all other blue objects) from cyan to purple.

Saturation Changes how vivid or pure the color is. For example, you can change a blue sky from grey to highly saturated blue.

Luminance Changes the brightness of the color range.

If you select Convert to Greyscale, you see only one nested tab:

Greyscale Mix Use controls in this tab to specify the contribution of each color range to the greyscale version of the image.

How to tone any greyscale image:

Use the controls in the Split Toning tab to color a greyscale image. You can add one color throughout the tonal range, such as a sepia appearance, or create a split tone result, in which a different color is applied to the shadows and the highlights. The extreme shadows and highlights remain black and white.

You can also apply special treatments, such as a cross-processed look, to a color image.

1. Select a greyscale image. (It can be an image that you converted to greyscale by selecting Convert to Greyscale in the HSL / Greyscale tab.)

2. In the Split Toning tab, adjust the Hue and Saturation properties for the highlights and shadows. Hue sets the color of the tone; Saturation sets the magnitude of the result.

3. Adjust the Balance control to balance the influence between the Highlight and Shadow

controls. Positive values increase the influence of the Highlight controls; negative values increase the influence of the Shadow controls.

How can you adjust the color or the tone using the Targeted Adjustment tool?

The Targeted Adjustment tool allows you to make tonal and color corrections by dragging directly on a photo. Using the Targeted Adjustment tool, you can drag down on a blue sky to de-saturate it, for example, or drag up on a red jacket to intensify its hue.

1. To make color adjustments with the Targeted Adjustment tool, click it in the toolbar and choose the type of correction you want to make: Hue, Saturation, Luminance, or Greyscale Mix. Then, drag in the image. Dragging up or right increases values; dragging down or left decreases values. Sliders for more than one color may be affected when you drag with the Targeted Adjustment tool. Selecting the Greyscale Mix Targeted Adjustment tool converts the image to greyscale.

2. To make tone curve adjustments using the Targeted Adjustment tool, click it in the toolbar and choose Parametric Curve. Then, drag in the image.

The Parametric Curve Targeted Adjustment tool adjusts the Highlights, Lights, Darks, or Shadows curve region based on the values in the image where you click. The keyboard shortcut T toggles the last Targeted Adjustment tool you used.

How to edit the HDR images in Camera Raw?

You can use the Basic tab controls to edit HDR images. The Basic tab Exposure control has an expanded range when working with HDR images (+10 to -10).

When you are done with editing, press Done or Open Image to open the image in Photoshop. The image opens as a 16-bit or 8-bit image, depending on how you have the Workflow Options set.

To open an HDR image in Camera Raw:

In Bridge, select the image and choose File > Open In Camera Raw. In mini-Bridge, right-click the image

(Ctrl-click on Mac) and choose Open With > Camera Raw.

For more information about HDR images, see High dynamic range images in Photoshop Help.

Understand the 'automatic perspective correction' feature in Camera Raw

Using an incorrect lens, or camera shake can cause the perspective of photographs to be tilted or skewed. The perspective may be distorted, and is more evident in photographs containing continuous vertical lines or geometric shapes.

Adobe Camera Raw has Upright modes - four settings that can be used to automatically fix perspective. The ability to manually apply corrections continues to be available. After applying an Upright mode, you can adjust the image further by manually modifying the available slider-based settings.

Note that, it is recommended that you apply any lens correction profiles available for your camera and lens combination, before you apply one of the four new presets. Applying the lens correction profile prepares the image to be analyzed better for distortion correction.

Learn about - how to manually correct the lens distortion using Upright presets?

1. Do one of the following:

    -   Open a camera raw file, or,

    -   With an image open in Photoshop, click Filter > Camera Raw Filter.

2. In the Camera Raw window, navigate to the Lens Corrections tab.

3. (Optional) In the Lens Corrections > Profile tab, select the Enable Lens Profile Corrections checkbox.

    Enabling Lens profile correction based on your camera and lens combination is highly recommended, before processing the photo with the Upright presets.

4. In Lens Corrections > Manual tab, there are four Upright modes available. Click a mode to apply the correction to the photo.

Auto: Applies a balanced set of perspective corrections.

Level: Applies perspective correction to ensure that the image is level.

Vertical: Applies level and vertical perspective corrections.

Full: Applies level, vertical and horizontal perspective corrections on the image.

Note that, While trying out the four Upright modes, if you select or clear the Enable Lens Profile Correction checkbox (Lens Correction > Profile), click the Reanalyze link below the Upright preset buttons.

Choose an Upright mode, and make further adjustments with the sliders

5. Cycle through the Upright modes until you find the most preferable setting.

The four Upright modes correct and manage distortion and perspective errors. There is no recommended or preferable setting. The best setting varies from one photo to another. Experiment with the four Upright modes before deciding on the best possible Upright mode for your photo.

6. Use the Transform sliders to make any further modifications, as necessary. A new slider (Aspect) has been introduced in Camera Raw.

- Move the Aspect slider left, to adjust the horizontal perspective of the photo.

- Move the Aspect slider right, to adjust the vertical perspective of the photo.

Image with no correction (left), image with Auto correction (middle), and image with Level correction (right).

Image with no correction (left), image with Vertical correction (middle), and image with Full correction (right).

Know about Radial Filter in Camera Raw:

To fully control, where a viewer's attention is drawn to on a photo, highlight the subject of the image. Some filters that create a vignette effect help you achieve that purpose. However, such filters require the main subject to be in the centre of the photo.

Radial filters in Adobe Camera Raw 8.0 enable you to direct attention to specific portions of the image to where you want the viewer to focus attention. For example, you can use the Radial Filter tool to draw an elliptical shape around the subject, and increase the exposure and clarity of the area within the shape to bring more attention to the subject.

The subject can be off-centre, or anywhere in the photography.

The main workflow to modify a photo with Radial Filters is outlined below:

1. Open a photo in the Adobe Camera Raw plug-in.

2. Identify one or more subjects that must attract the viewer's attention

3. Set up:

    • (Optional) A Radial filter to weaken focus on the background

    • A Radial filter to highlight the subject

- Additional Radial filters, if you have more than one subject to highlight

The subject of the photo is not clearly visible in the original photo (left), but is highlighted using a Radial Filter (right)

How to apply the Radial Filter to enhance a photo:

1. Do one of the following:

    - Open a camera raw file, or,

    - With an image open in Photoshop, click Filter > Camera Raw Filter.

2. Select the Radial Filter tool from the toolbar.

    Press J to toggle the Radial Filter tool.

3. Use the New and Edit radio button options to choose whether you want to create a filter, or edit an existing filter.

4. Do one of the following:

    - To create a Radial Filter, click and drag the mouse across the region, and draw a circular or elliptical shape. This shape determines the area that is affected or

114

excluded from the alterations you are about to perform.

- To edit a Radial Filter, click any of the grey handles on the photo. When selected, the handle turns red.

5. To determine what area of the photo is modified, choose an Effect option (located below the sliders).

- Outside. All modifications are applied outside the selected area.

- Inside. All modifications are applied to the selected area.

6. Adjust the size (width and height) and orientation of the Radial Filter added. Select a filter, and:

- Click and drag the centre of the filter to move and reposition it.

- Hover the pointer any of the four filter handles, and when the pointer icon changes, click and drag to change the size of the filter.

- Hover the pointer close to the edge of the filter, and when the pointer icon changes, click and drag the edge of the filter to change the orientation.

The Radial Filter is represented by an elliptical marquee

7. Use the sliders to modify the selected Radial Filter area. The Feather slider adjusts the falloff of the applied effect.

The Radial Filter tool options allow you to apply effects to an elliptical mask.

8. Follow steps 3 through 6 to continue adding or editing Radial Filters.

9. Clear the Overlay checkbox, to show how the finished photo appears. If you want to delete all the Radial Filters and start from scratch, click Clear All (this action cannot be undone).

10. Use the Mask option to enable mask visualization. Alternatively, press Y to toggle the Mask setting.

How to modify the Radial Filter instance using brush controls:

You can modify Radial Filter masks using brush controls. Once you've added a mask, to access brush controls, select the Brush option next to New/Edit. Alternatively, press Shift + K.

As appropriate, use the + and - brushes. Brush controls for Radial Filter masks

The shortcuts (Keyboard) and modifiers for Radial Filter tool:

New adjustments

- Press and hold Shift + drag, to create an adjustment that is constrained to a circle

- While dragging, press and hold the spacebar to move the ellipse; release the spacebar to resume defining the shape of the new adjustment

Editing adjustments

- While dragging inside an adjustment to move it, press and hold the Shift key to constrain the movement in the horizontal or vertical direction

- While dragging one of the four handles to resize an adjustment, press and hold the Shift key, to preserve the aspect ratio of the adjustment shape.

- While dragging the boundary of an adjustment to rotate it, press and hold the Shift key to snap the rotation to 15-degree increments.

- While an adjustment is selected, press the X key to flip the effect direction (for example, from outside to inside)

Deleting adjustments

- While an adjustment is selected, press the Delete key to delete the adjustment

- Press Option/Alt + click an existing adjustment to delete it

Adjustments with maximum coverage

- Press Command/Control and double-click on an empty area, to create an adjustment that is centered and covers the cropped image area

- Press Command/Control and double-click within an existing adjustment, to expand that adjustment to cover the cropped image area

Feature- About the Enhanced Spot Removal Tool in Camera Raw:

The Spot Removal tool in Camera Raw lets you repair a selected area of an image by sampling from a different area of the same image. The tool is similar to the Healing Brush available in Photoshop. The default BEHAVIOUR for the Spot Removal tool is to be able to mark areas to touch up, by dragging the brush across the photo. For example, remove a portion of the wire (connecting the helmet and the overhead wire) that is distracting the view of the blue sky. Using the Spot Removal tool on a raw image means that you are processing the raw image data directly. Working with raw image data directly can provide cleaner matches for retouching (healing or cloning) actions. Also, since any edits and modifications to camera raw images are stored in sidecar files, this process is non-destructive.

The zip line that appears to be connecting the wire and the helmet (image left) has been removed (image right)

Steps to use the Spot Removal tool:

1. Do one of the following:

   • Open a camera raw file, or,

   • With an image open in Photoshop, click Filter > Camera Raw Filter.

2. Select the Spot Removal tool from the toolbar.

3. Select one of the following from the Type menu:

   Heal - Matches the texture, lighting, and shading of the sampled area to the selected area. Clone- Applies the sampled area of the image to the selected area.

4. (Optional) In the Spot Removal tool options area under the Histogram, drag the Size slider

to specify the size of the area that the Spot Removal tool affects.

Use the bracket keys on your keyboard to change brush size

- •Left bracket ([), reduces the tool radius size

- Right bracket (]), increases the tool radius size.

5. In the photo, click and drag the part of the photo to retouch.

- A red-and-white marquee area (red handle) designates your selection.

- A green-and-white marquee area (green handle) designates the sampled area.

Identify the part of the image to heal, and then use the Spot Removal tool, to paint the area. Use the green and red handles (image right) to reposition the selected and sample areas

6. (Optional) To change the sampled area that is selected by default, do one of the following:

- Automatically. Click the handle of a selected area, and press the forward slash key (/). A new area is sampled.

Press the forward slash key until you find a sample area that fits best.

- Manually. Use the green handle to reposition the sampled area.

When you select larger portions of an image using longer strokes, the right sample area match is not found immediately. To experiment with various options, click the forward slash (/) and the tool auto-samples more areas for you.

7. To remove all the adjustments made using the Spot Removal tool, click Clear All.

Keyboard shortcuts and modifiers

Circular spot:

- Control/Command + click to create a circular spot; drag to set the source of the spot.

- Command/Control + Option/Alt + click to create a circular spot; drag to set the size of the spot.

Rectangular selection:

- Click Option/Alt + drag to define a rectangular selection. All spots within that selection (highlighted in red) are deleted once the mouse is released.

Extend a selected area or spot:

- Shift + click to extend an existing selected spot in "connect the dots" fashion.

Delete a selected area or spot:

- Select a red or green handle, and press Delete to delete a selected adjustment.

- Press Option/Alt and click a handle to delete it.

How to clean up photo with the Visualize Spots feature:

While working on a computer screen, you may be able to identify and remove most visible spots or imperfections.

However, when you print a photo at its full resolution, the printed output may contain many imperfections that were not visible on a computer screen. These imperfections could be of many types - dust on a camera sensor, blemishes on a model's skin in a portrait, tiny wisps of clouds on blue skies. At full resolution, these imperfections are visually distracting.

The new Visualize Spots feature lets you search for imperfections that may not be immediately visible. When you select the Visualize Spots checkbox (found in the options for the Spot Removal tool), the image is inverted. You can then use the Spot Removal tool in the Visualize Spots mode, to clean up the image further.

The Visualize Spots checkbox is a Spot Removal tool option

1. Do one of the following:

   • Open a camera raw file, or,

   • With an image open in Photoshop CC, click Filter > Camera Raw Filter.

2. Select the Spot Removal tool from the toolbar, and then select the Visualize Spots checkbox. The image is inverted, and the outlines of the elements of the image are

visible. Above, Visualize Spots view is off, and unnecessary elements like wispy clouds (left) have been removed (right)

3. Use the Visualize Spots slider to vary the contrast threshold of the inverted image. Move the slider to different contrast levels, to view imperfections like sensor dust, dots, or other unwanted elements. When the Spot Visualization checkbox is selected, to change the visualization threshold:

   - •Increase: Press. (period)

   - Increase (in larger steps): Press Shift +

   - Reduce: Press ,

   - Reduce (in larger steps): Press Shift + ,

4. Use the Spot Removal tool to clone or heal out unwanted elements in the photo. Uncheck the Visualize Spots checkbox to view the resulting image.

5. Repeat steps 2, 3, and 4.

Know how to make the local adjustments in the Camera Raw:

What are local adjustments?

The controls in the image adjustment tabs of Camera Raw affect the color and tone of an entire photo. To adjust a specific area of a photo, like dodging and burning, use the Adjustment Brush tool and the Graduated Filter tool in Camera Raw.

The Adjustment Brush tool lets you selectively apply Exposure, Brightness, Clarity, and other adjustments by "painting" them onto the photo.

The Graduated Filter tool lets you apply the same types of adjustments gradually across a region of a photo. You can make the region as wide or as narrow as you like.

You can apply both types of local adjustments to any photo. You can synchronize local adjustment settings across multiple selected images. You can also create local adjustment presets so that you can quickly reapply an effect that you use frequently.

Getting local adjustments "right" in Camera Raw takes some experimentation. The recommended workflow is to select a tool and specify its options, and then apply the adjustment to the photo. Then you can go back and edit that adjustment, or apply a new one.

Like all other adjustments applied in Camera Raw, local adjustments are non destructive. They are never permanently applied to the photo. Local adjustments are saved with an image in an XMP sidecar file or in the Camera Raw database, depending on what's specified in Camera Raw preferences.

How can you apply local adjustments with Adjustment Brush tool in Camera Raw?

1. Select the Adjustment Brush tool from the toolbar (or press K). Camera Raw opens the Adjustment Brush tool options under the Histogram and sets the mask mode to New.

2. Choose the type of adjustment you want to make in the Adjustment Brush tool options by dragging an effects slider.

   Note that, the effects that are available depend on whether you are working in Process Version 2012, 2010, or 2003, as noted.

To update a photo to PV2012, click the exclamation-point icon in the lower-right corner of the image preview.

Temp (PV2012): Adjusts the color temperature of an area of the image, making it warmer or cooler. A graduated filter temperature effect can improve images captured in mixed-lighting conditions.

Tint (PV2012): Compensates for a green or magenta color cast.

Exposure (All): Sets the overall image brightness. Applying an Exposure local correction can achieve results similar to traditional dodging and burning.

Highlights (PV2012): Recovers detail in overexposed highlight areas of an image.

Shadows (PV2012): Recovers detail in underexposed shadow areas of an image.

Brightness (PV2010 and PV2003): Adjusts the image brightness, with a greater effect in the mild tones.

Contrast (All): Adjusts the image contrast, with a greater effect in the midtones.

Saturation (All): Changes the vividness or purity of the color.

Clarity (All): Adds depth to an image by increasing local contrast.

Sharpness (All): Enhances edge definition to bring out details in a photo. A negative value blurs details.

Noise Reduction (PV2012): Reduces luminance noise, which can become apparent when shadow areas are opened.

Moiré Reduction (PV2012): Removes moiré artifacts, or color aliasing.

Defringe (PV2012): Removes fringe colors along edges. See Remove local color fringes.

Color (All): Applies a tint to the selected area. Select the hue by clicking the color sample box to the right of the effect name.

Click the Plus icons (+) or the Minus icons (-) to increase or decrease the effect by a preset amount. Click multiple times to select a stronger adjustment. Double-click the slider to reset the effect to zero.

3. Specify brush options:

    Size Specifies the diameter of the brush tip, in pixels.

    Feather Controls the hardness of the brush stroke.

    Flow Controls the rate of application of the adjustment.

    Density Controls the amount of transparency in the stroke.

    Auto Mask Confines brush strokes to areas of similar color.

    Show Mask Toggles visibility of the mask overlay in the image preview.

4. Move the Adjustment Brush tool over the image.

    The cross hair indicates the application point. The solid circle indicates the brush size. The black-and-white dashed circle indicates the feather amount.

Note that, if the Feather is set to 0, the black-and-white circle indicates the brush size. With very small feather amounts, the solid circle may not be visible.

5. Paint with the Adjustment Brush tool in the area of the image that you want to adjust.

    When you release the mouse, a pin icon appears at the application point. In the Adjustment Brush tool options, the mask mode changes to Add.

6. (Optional) Refine the adjustment by doing any of the following:

    • Drag any of the effect sliders in the Adjustment Brush tool options to customize the effect in the image.

    • Press V to hide or show the pin icon.

    • To toggle visibility of the mask overlay, use the Show Mask option, press Y, or position the pointer over the pin icon.

    To customize the color of the mask overlay, click the color swatch next to the Show Mask option. Then, choose a new color from the Color Picker.

- To undo part of the adjustment, click Erase in the Adjustment Brush tool options and paint over the adjustment.

To create an eraser brush that has different characteristics from the current Adjustment Brush tool, click the Local Adjustment Settings menu button and choose Separate Eraser Size. Then, specify the Size, Feather, Flow, and Density you want for the eraser.

- Remove the adjustment completely by selecting the pin and pressing Delete.

- Press Ctrl+Z (in windows) or Command+Z (in Mac OS) to undo your last adjustment.

- Click Clear All at the bottom of the tool options to remove all Adjustment Brush tool adjustments and set the mask mode to New.

7. (Optional) Click New to apply an additional Adjustment Brush tool adjustment, and refine it as desired using the techniques in step 6.

Note that, when working with multiple Adjustment Brush adjustments, make sure you're in Add mode to switch between them. Click a pin icon to select that adjustment and refine it.

How to modify a Graduated Filter instance using the brush controls?

You can modify Graduated Filter masks using brush controls. Once you've added a mask, to access brush controls, select the Brush option next to New/Edit. Alternatively, with a Graduated Filter instance selected, press Shift + K. As appropriate, use the + and - brushes.

Note that, the add/remove functionality is available only to Photoshop CC customers using Camera Raw 8.5 or later.

Refine the filter by doing any of the following:

- Drag any of the effect sliders in the Graduated Filter tool options to customize the filter.

- Toggle visibility of the guide overlays by selecting the Overlay option (or press V).

- Drag the green or red dot to freely expand, contract, and rotate the effect.

- Drag the black-and-white dotted line to shift the effect.

- Position the pointer over the green-and-white or red-and-white dotted line, near the green or red dot, until a double-pointing arrow appears. Then, drag to expand or contract the effect at that end of the range.

- Position the pointer over the green-and-white or red-and-white dotted line, away from the green or red dot, until a curved double-pointing arrow appears. Then, drag to rotate the effect.

- Remove the filter by pressing Delete.

- Press Ctrl+Z (in windows) or Command+Z (in Mac OS) to undo your last adjustment.

- Use the Mask option to enable mask visualization. Alternatively, press Y to toggle the Mask setting.

- Click Clear All at the bottom of the tool options to remove all Graduated Filter tool effects and set the mask mode to New.

(Optional) Click New to apply an additional Graduated Filter tool effect, and refine it as desired using the techniques in step 4.

Note that, while working with multiple Graduated Filter effects, click an overlay to select that effect and refine it.

How to save and apply the local adjustment presets?

You can save local adjustments as presets so that you can quickly apply the effects to other images. You create, select, and manage local adjustment presets using the Camera Raw Settings menu in the Adjustment Brush or Graduated

Filter tool options. You apply local adjustment presets using the Adjustment Brush tool or the Graduated Filter tool

Note that, Local adjustments cannot be saved with Camera Raw image presets.

In the Adjustment Brush or Graduated Filter tool options in the Camera Raw dialog box, click the Camera Raw Settings menu button. Then, choose one of the following commands:

New Local Correction Setting Saves the current local adjustment effect settings as a preset. Type a name and click OK. Saved presets appear in the Local Adjustment Settings menu and can be applied to any image that is opened in Camera Raw.

Delete "preset name" Deletes the selected local adjustment preset.

Rename "preset name" Renames the selected local adjustment preset. Type a name and click OK.

Preset name Select a preset to apply its settings with the Adjustment Brush tool or the Graduated Filter tool.

When using local adjustment presets, keep in mind the following:

- Only one local adjustment preset can be selected at a time.

- When applying a local adjustment preset with the Adjustment Brush tool, you can still customize the brush options, including Size, Feather, Flow, and Density. The preset applies the effect settings at the specified brush size.

- After a local adjustment preset is applied, you can refine it as desired.

- The same effect settings are available for the Adjustment Brush tool and the Graduated Filter tool. As a result, local adjustment presets can be applied using either tool, regardless of which tool was used to create the preset.

What is sharpening and noise reduction in Camera Raw?

Sharpen photos

The sharpening controls on the Detail tab adjust edge definition in the image. The Adjustment Brush tool and Graduated Filter tool use the Radius, Detail, and Masking values when local sharpening is applied. Use the Apply Sharpening To option in the Camera Raw preferences to specify whether sharpening is applied to all images or just to previews.

To open preferences from within Camera Raw, click the Open Preferences Dialog button in the toolbar.

1. Zoom the preview image to at least 100%.

2. In the Detail tab, adjust any of these controls:

   Amount: Adjusts edge definition. Increase the Amount value to increase sharpening. A value of zero (0) turns off sharpening. In general, set Amount to a lower value for cleaner images. The adjustment is a variation of Unsharp Mask, which locates pixels that differ from surrounding pixels based on the threshold you specify and increases the pixels' contrast by the amount you specify. When opening a camera raw image file, the Camera Raw plug-in calculates the threshold to use based on camera model, ISO, and exposure compensation.

   Radius: Adjusts the size of the details that sharpening is applied to. Photos with fine details generally need a lower setting. Photos with larger details can use a larger radius. Using too large a radius generally results in unnatural looking results.

Detail: Adjusts how much high-frequency information is sharpened in the image and how much the sharpening process emphasizes edges. Lower settings primarily sharpen edges to remove blurring. Higher values are useful for making the textures in the image more pronounced.

Masking: Controls an edge mask. With a setting of zero (0), everything in the image receives the same amount of sharpening. With a setting of 100, sharpening is mostly restricted to those areas near the strongest edges. Press Alt (in windows) or Option (in Mac OS) while dragging this slider to see the areas to be sharpened (white) versus the areas masked out (black).

3. (Optional) To apply the newest sharpening algorithms to images; click the Update To Current Process (2012) button in the lower-right corner of the image preview.

How to reduce the noise:

The Noise Reduction section of the Detail tab has controls for reducing image noise, the extraneous visible artifacts that degrade image quality. Image noise includes luminance (greyscale) noise, which makes an image look grainy, and chroma (color) noise, which is visible as colored artifacts in the image. Photos taken with high ISO speeds or less sophisticated digital cameras can have noticeable noise.

Note that, when making noise reduction adjustments, first zoom in on the preview image to at least 100% to see the noise reduction previewed. Adjusting the Color and Color Detail sliders reduces chroma noise while preserving color detail (lower right). Note that, if the Luminance Detail, Luminance Contrast, and Color Detail sliders are dimmed, click the Update To Current Process (2012) button in the lower-right corner of the image.

Luminance: Reduces luminance noise.

Luminance Detail: Controls the luminance noise threshold. It is useful for noisy photos. Higher values preserve more detail but can produce noisier results. Lower values produce cleaner results but also remove some detail.

Luminance Contrast: Controls the luminance contrast. It is useful for noisy photos. Higher values preserve contrast but can produce noisy blotches or mottling. Lower values produce smoother results but can also have less contrast.

Color: Reduces color noise.

Color Detail: Controls the color noise threshold. Higher values protect thin, detailed color edges but can result in colors pecking. Lower values remove color speckles but can result in color bleeding.

For video tutorials about reducing noise in Camera Raw, see:

- Better noise reduction in Photoshop® CS5 by Matt Kloskowski

- Lens correction and noise reduction with Adobe® Camera Raw by Russell Brown

- Photoshop CS5 - Camera Raw 6.0 by Justin Seeley

Know about Correcting lens distortions in Camera Raw:

What is lens correction?

Camera lenses can exhibit different types of defects at certain focal lengths, f-stops, and focus distances. You can correct for these apparent distortions and aberrations using the Lens Corrections tab of the Camera Raw dialog box.

Vignetting causes the edges, especially the corners, of an image to be darker than the center. Use controls in the Lens Vignetting section of the Lens Corrections tab to compensate for vignetting.

Barrel distortion causes straight lines to appear to bow outward. Pincushion distortion causes straight lines to appear to bend inward. Chromatic aberration is caused by the failure of the lens to focus different colors to the same spot. In one type of chromatic aberration, the image from each color of light is in focus, but each image is a slightly different size. Another type of chromatic artifact affects the edges of specular highlights, such as those found when light reflects off water or polished metal. This situation usually results in a purple fringe around each specular highlight.

Below are the two images which show the effect of the lens correction. The image on the left is before the correction is done and that on the right is the final image after correction.

The options in the nested Profile tab of the Lens Corrections tab of the Camera Raw dialog box correct distortions in common camera lenses. The profiles are based on Exit metadata that identifies the camera and lens that captured the photo, and the profiles compensate accordingly.

1. In the nested Profile tab of the Lens Corrections tab, select Enable Lens Profile Corrections.

2. If Camera Raw does not find a suitable profile automatically, select a Make, Model, and Profile.

   Note that, some cameras have only one lens, and some lenses have only one profile. The lenses that are available depend on whether you're adjusting a raw or a non-raw file.

3. If desired, customize the correction applied by the profile by using the Amount sliders: Distortion The default value 100 applies 100% of the distortion correction in the profile. Values over 100 apply greater correction to the distortion; values under 100 apply less correction to the distortion.

Chromatic Aberration: The default value 100 applies 100% of the chromatic aberration correction in the profile. Values over 100 apply greater correction to color fringing; values under 100 apply less correction to color fringing.

Vignetting: The default value 100 applies 100% of the vignetting correction in the profile. Values over 100 apply greater correction to vignetting; values under 100 apply less correction to vignetting.

4. (Optional) To apply your changes to the default profile, choose Setup > Save New Lens Profile Defaults.

What does it mean to correct image perspective and lens flaws automatically?

Transform and vignette corrections can be applied to original and cropped photos. Lens vignettes adjust exposure values to brighten dark corners.

1. Click the nested Manual tab of the Lens Corrections tab of the Camera Raw dialog box.

2. Under Transform, adjust any of the following:

   Distortion: Drag to the right to correct barrel distortion and straighten lines that bend away from the center. Drag to the left to correct pincushion distortion and straighten lines that bend toward the center.

   Vertical: Corrects perspective caused by tilting the camera up or down. Makes vertical lines appear parallel.

   Horizontal: Corrects perspective caused by angling the camera left or right. Makes horizontal lines appear parallel.

   Rotate: Corrects for camera tilt.

   Scale: Adjusts the image scale up or down. It helps to remove empty areas caused by perspective corrections and distortions and it displays areas of the image that extend beyond the crop boundary.

3. Under Chromatic Aberration, adjust any of the following:

Fix Red/Cyan Fringe: Adjusts the size of the red channel relative to the green channel.

Fix Blue/Yellow Fringe: Adjusts the size of the blue channel relative to the green channel.

Zoom in on an area that contains very dark or black detail against a very light or white background. Look for color fringing. To more clearly see the color fringing, press Alt (in windows) or Option (in Mac OS) as you move a slider to hide any color fringe corrected by the other color slider.

Defringe: Choose All Edges to correct color fringing for all edges, including any sharp change in color values. If choosing All Edges results in thin grey lines or other undesired effects, choose Highlight Edges to correct color fringing only in the edges of highlighting where fringing is most likely to occur. Choose Off to turn off defringing.

4. Under Lens Vignetting adjust the following:

    Amount: Move the Amount slider to the right (positive values) to lighten the corners of the photo. Move the slider to the left (negative values) to darken the corners of the photo.

    Midpoint: Drag the Midpoint slider to the left (lower value) to apply the Amount adjustment to a larger area away from the corners. Drag the slider to the right (higher value) to restrict the adjustment to an area closer to the corners.

Lesson 9: The Adobe Bridge

Basic Concept

Adobe Bridge is something that helps you organize your assets. By assets, I mean the files you use to create for printing, publishing on the web or making videos. It helps you manage and organize them in a classified manner, making it easy for the user to use them and create better contents.

The required assets, according to use, can be dragged into your layouts, projects and various compositions as needed. The assets can also be dragged to Adobe Bridge in order to preview files or to add metadata that makes the files easier to locate. Metadata is the required file information.

While creating content, say for printing, or say some making some video for publishing on the web, which is already a very hefty task, as you need to use lots of brain in deciding what to clip from what file and how to merge to the ongoing content file or something like this. Now, suppose we require four to five files from where we require content for our files. While creating the content, you will have to open each file, be it an Adobe file or a non- Adobe files separately and then closes it. The task gets bulky and puzzles you up while creating. The Adobe Bridge finds an importance here. Using Adobe Bridge, in simple words, you can accumulate all the required content files at a single place and easily use them for work.

The access of adobe and non-adobe files is a feature of great use. Most of the times, we require files which are non –adobe, I mean files which are neither PSD nor PDF, in that case, we get puzzled up regarding how to open and clip contents from the same. The task of separately going for each of them irritates the user. The Adobe Bridge has a remarkable use in that case.

I will explain the complete detail about ADOBE BRIDGE in the upcoming theory and after studying this lesson, you will be able to know how to install the ADOBE BRIDGE, the use, features of the same. The differences of the same from older and previous versions and almost, all useful information about it shall be discussed. All you need to do is to carefully and calmly read the contents and follow the steps altogether. Not just reading would help you, but practicing together and time to time shall bring perfection in you. Just after you get handy with the feature, you shall start liking it and use it to utmost perfection.

What kind of files can be stored in Adobe Bridge?

Adobe Bridge keeps the native Adobe files such as PSD AND PDF. It also keeps non-Adobe files, which you may need for an easy access while creating some content for printing or publishing on web whatever.

The ability to store both kinds of files makes the feature an exceptionally helpful one. The non- adobe files find their use equally as the adobe ones while creating contents.

Basic features of Adobe Bridge

Adobe Bridge has many features that are of great use to users. Here, I am listing below some of the major utility features-

EASY BROWSING OF FILES:

This is the most basic feature of ABODE BRIDGE. I have been explaining it to you since the beginning. This involves browsing of files from Adobe Bridge. The following are the basic functions you can perform to files in the bridge-

- You can search, view, sort, filter, manage, and process images, page layout, PDF, and dynamic media files.

- You can also use Adobe Bridge to rename, move, and delete files.

- You can edit metadata, which is the important file information.

- You can rotate images and run batch commands.

- You can also view files and data imported from your digital still or video camera. See View and manage files.

What is Mini Bridge?

The following are the basic functional features of the Mini bridge-

- It helps you browse and manage your assets using the Mini Bridge panel in Adobe Photoshop, Adobe InDesign, and Adobe In-Copy. These are all separate software that involves the use of the mini bridge feature.

- Mini Bridge communicates with Adobe Bridge to create thumbnails and keep files up-to-date. This is a very vital feature as keeping files up to date is of utmost importance.

- Mini Bridge lets you work with files more easily within the host application. The ease factor makes a room for its high usage.

Opening of camera raw files:

The features listed below tell the importance of ADOBE BRIDGE regarding opening of Camera raw files-

- If you have Adobe PHOTOSHOP, or say, Adobe LIGHTROOM, or Adobe Creative Suite installed in your system, you can open camera raw files using the Adobe Bridge and save them there itself.

- You can also edit the images directly in the Camera Raw dialogue box without starting Photoshop or LIGHTROOM, and copy the settings from one image to another image.

- If you do not have Photoshop installed in your system, you can still preview the camera raw files in Adobe Bridge. This feature lets you see the files without Photoshop.

Feature - Color management:

The next significant feature of ADOBE BRIDGE is color management. If you have a Creative Cloud membership, or an edition of Adobe Creative Suite 6 or CS5 installed in our system, you can use Adobe Bridge to synchronize color settings across color-managed Adobe Creative Suite components. This synchronization ensures that colors look the same in all Adobe Creative Suite components. The color management feature is of utmost importance in several fields where matching the right tones of color is mandatory. The people who marginally require highly precise specifications are a big fan of the tool.

These are the major features of the ADOBE BRIDGE. There are many other applications and features of the same, which you shall understand yourself after reading the complete lesson. It is an advice that you shall go through the features listed above closely in order to utilize the tool you learn here in maximum weightage. Now we will go through other details regarding the tool.

Different ways to start Adobe Bridge:

You can open ADOBE BRIDGE in a multiple ways. The major ways of starting are as listed below-

1. You can choose to start Adobe Bridge from an Adobe product:

   For opening through this method, you can perform either of the following operation:

   • Choose File -> Browse or File -> Browse 'In Bridge' (as per availability).

   Note that, In After-Effects, or Premiere Pro, after you use File -> Browse 'In Bridge' to start Adobe Bridge, double-click on a file will open or import the file into that Creative Suite 5 component, not into the native application.

   For example, if you choose File -> Browse 'In Bridge' in Adobe Premiere Pro and then double-click a Photoshop file, the file adds to the Premiere Pro Project panel, rather than getting open in Photoshop.

- Click the Adobe Bridge button in the application bar.

2. You can choose to return to the last open Adobe product from the Adobe Bridge:

This is an easy and most commonly used method. For using this method, you can perform operations listed below-

- Choose File -> Return to [Component] or click the Return to [Component] button in the application bar.

3. You can choose to switch to Adobe Bridge from Mini Bridge as well:

This is applicable in Photoshop, InDesign and 'In-Copy'. To open through this method, follow-

- Click the Open Bridge button at the top of the Mini Bridge panel and you shall get it opened.

4. You can choose to start Adobe Bridge automatically:

You can configure your Adobe Bridge to run automatically in the background every time you log in. You will not have to open it every time after you configure your system for this. Running Adobe Bridge in the background consumes fewer system resources until you are ready to use it. The instructions to configure your system for the same are as follows-

To configure Adobe Bridge to open automatically in the background at login, do perform one of the following:

- The first time you launch 'ADOBE BRIDGE', click on 'Yes' when asked if you want to launch Adobe Bridge automatically at login.

- In the Advanced panel of the Adobe Bridge Preferences dialogue box, choose Start Bridge at Login.

- In Windows, when Adobe Bridge is already open, right-click the Adobe Bridge system tray icon and choose Start Bridge At Login.

Any of these actions shall configure your system for an automatic start of the ADOBE BRIDGE. Note that, when Adobe Bridge is running in the background, it may interfere with the installation of other Adobe applications and plug-ins. If this happens, quit Adobe Bridge.

5. You can choose to start Adobe Bridge directly:

The Adobe Bridge can also be open in both windows and in Mac 'OS' directly like any other software you open. The instructions for the same follows-

• In Windows,

Choose Adobe Bridge from the Start -> Programs menu to open.

• In Mac OS,

 Double-click on the Adobe Bridge icon located in the Applications/Adobe Bridge folder to open.

6. You can choose to hide or show Adobe Bridge:

The Adobe Bridge has a special feature of showing or hiding itself. The instructions for using the same are as follows--

In Windows, Do perform any of the following in order to switch between operational modes:-

- Right-click on the Adobe Bridge icon in the system tray and choose Show Bridge to open the application.

- Choose File -> Hide to run Adobe Bridge in the background.

- Right-click on the Adobe Bridge icon in the system tray and choose Hide Bridge to run Adobe Bridge in the background.

In Mac OS, Perform any of the following to switch between operational modes:

- Click on the Adobe Bridge icon in the Dock and choose Show or Hide.

- In Adobe Bridge, choose Adobe Bridge ->Hide Adobe Bridge to run Adobe Bridge in the background.

These were the different ways to start the Adobe Bridge. To know about any software, you must initially know about all the possible ways of starting the application. You must read it carefully to help yourself open the software from any of the above listed methods you feel handy with it. Now, we shall proceed with other details about it.

Understanding the Adobe Bridge workspace in detail:

After you learn to start the ADOBE BRIDGE, the next main task is to understand the workspace that opens up. Now, I shall go into the detailed overview of the workspace and you should go through this carefully to understand all the buttons and features of the same.

The Adobe Bridge workspace consists mainly of three columns that contain various panels as you can see in the figure. Now, see what you can do to the overview.

You can adjust the Adobe Bridge workspace by moving or resizing these panels.

You can create custom workspaces or select from several preconfigured Adobe Bridge workspaces.

Now, follow the main components of the Adobe Bridge workspace:

- Path bar:

It displays the path to the folder you are viewing and it allows you to navigate the directory also.

- Application bar:

  It provides the buttons for essential tasks, such as navigating the folder hierarchy, switching workspaces, and searching for files etc.

- Favorites panel:

  It gives you a quick access to frequently browsed folders.

- Folders panel:

  It shows the folder hierarchy. You may use it to navigate folders.

- Preview panel:

  It shows a preview of the selected file or say, files. The previews are separate from, and typically larger than, the thumbnail images displayed in the Content panel. You can reduce or enlarge the preview by resizing the panel.

- Filter panel:

    It helps you sort and filter all the files that appear in the Content panel.

- Content panel:

    It displays the files specified by the navigational menu buttons, path bar, favorite panel, folders panel, or collections panel.

- Collections panel:

    It lets you create, locate, and open the collections and smart collections.

- Export panel:

    In CS6 and CS5, you can save photos as JPEG for web uploads.

- Metadata panel:

    This panel contains metadata information for the selected file. If multiple files are selected, shared data such as keywords, date created, and exposure setting is listed in this panel.

- Output panel:

In CS6 and CS5, it contains options for creating PDF documents and HTML or Flash® web galleries. It only appears when the Output workspace is selected.

- Keywords panel:

   It helps you organize your images by attaching keywords to them.

How to manage and select workspaces:

The Adobe Bridge workspace is a certain configuration or a layout of panels. You can select a preconfigured workspace or a custom workspace that you have previously saved. By saving the various Adobe Bridge workspaces, you can work in and quickly switch between the different layouts. For instance, use one workspace to sort new photos and another to work with footage files from an After Effects composition.

Adobe Bridge provides with the following pre-configured workspaces:

Metadata:

It displays the Content panel in List view, along with the Favorites, Metadata, Filter, and Export panels.

Essentials:

It displays the Favorites, Folders, Filter, Collections, Export, Content, Preview, Metadata, and Keywords panels.

Output:

It displays the Favorites, folders, content, preview, and output panels. The workspace is available when the Adobe Output Module start up script is being selected in the Adobe Bridge Preferences.

Keywords:

It shows the Content panel in Details view, along with the Favorites, Keywords, Filter, and Export panels. Note that, In Mac OS, press Command+F5 to load the Keywords workspace starts Mac OS Voice-Over by default. To load the Preview workspace by using the keyboard shortcut, first disable the Voice-Over shortcut in Mac OS Keyboard Shortcuts preferences. For instructions, see Mac OS Help.

Light Table:

It displays only the Content panel. Files are at a display in Thumbnails view.

Filmstrip:

It displays the thumbnails in a scrolling horizontal row (in the Content panel) along with a preview of the currently selected item (in the Preview panel). Also displays the Favorites, Folders, Filter, Collections, and Export panels.

Preview:

It displays a large Preview panel; a narrow, vertical Content panel in Thumbnails view; and the Favorites, Folders, Filter, Collections, and Export panels.

Folders:

It shows the Content panel in Thumbnails view, along with the Favorites, Folders, and Export panels.

- For selecting a workspace, choose Window -> Workspace, and then choose the desired workspace. Otherwise you may, click one of the workspace buttons in the Adobe Bridge application bar.

- Now, drag the vertical bar to the left of the workspace buttons to show more or fewer buttons. Drag the buttons to rearrange their order.

- For saving the current layout as a workspace, choose Window -> Workspace -> New Workspace. In the New Workspace dialog box, you can enter a name for the workspace, specify options, and then click Save.

- For deleting or restoring a custom workspace, choose Window -> Workspace, and then choose one of the following commands:

Delete Workspace:

It deletes the saved workspace. Now, choose the workspace from the Workspace menu in the Delete Workspace dialog box, and click Delete.

Reset Workspace:

It restores the currently selected saved workspace to its default settings.

Reset Standard Workspace:

It restores the default settings for the Adobe pre-defined workspaces (Essentials, Output, etc.)

How can you adjust the panels in the Workspace?

The adjustment of panels in the workspace is quite possible. You can adjust the Adobe Bridge window by moving or resizing its panels. However, you cannot move panels outside the Adobe Bridge window but can move them inside.

Perform any of the following operation to adjust panels accordingly:

- Drag the vertical divider bar between the panels and the Content panel to resize the panels or Content panel.

- Drag the horizontal divider bar between the panels to make them larger or smaller.

- Drag a panel you want to move by its tab into another panel.

- Select a Window, followed by the name of the panel you want to display or hide.

- Press Tab to show or hide all panels except the centre panel (the centre panel varies depending on the workspace you have chosen).

- Right-click in Windows or Control-click In Mac OS on the panel tab and choose the name of the panel you want to display.

How to work with the 'Favorites menu' in Workspace:

To work with the Favorites menu, follow the instructions as follows-

- To specify the 'Favorites' preferences,

    Choose Edit -> Preferences in Windows or Adobe Bridge CS6 -> Preferences in Mac OS. Click General, and select desired options in the Favorites Items area of the Preferences dialog box.

- To add items to Favorites menu, do perform one of the following:

- Drag a file or folder to the Favorites panel from Windows Explorer in Windows, the Finder in Mac OS, or the Content or Folders panel of Adobe Bridge.

- Select a file, folder, or collection in the Adobe Bridge and choose File -> Add to Favorites.

To remove an item from the Favorites panel, select it and choose File -> Remove from Favorite. Otherwise, you may right-click (in Windows) or Control-click (in

Mac OS) the item and choose Remove from Favorites from the context menu.

How can you adjust brightness and the colors?

You can brighten or darken the Adobe Bridge background and specify accent colors in General preferences. This feature adds color effects to the background to make it look attractive.

To open the preferences, choose Edit -> Preferences (in Windows) or Adobe Bridge -> Preferences (in Mac OS).

To brighten or darken the background, you can go to the General panel of the Preferences dialog box and do the following:

- FEATURE - Drag the User Interface Brightness slider to make the Adobe Bridge background darker or lighter.

- FEATURE - Drag the Image Backdrop slider to make the background of slide shows and of the Content and Preview panels darker or lighter.

- FEATURE - To specify the accent colors, go to the General panel of the Preferences dialog box and choose a color from the Accent Color menu.

How can you enable start-up scripts?

You can disable or enable the start-up scripts in Adobe Bridge preferences. The listed Scripts vary depending on the Creative Suite components you have installed in your system. You should disable start-up scripts to improve the performance or to resolve the incompatibilities between scripts.

The instructions for the same are as follows-

1. Choose Edit -> Preferences (in Windows) or Adobe Bridge -> Preferences (in Mac OS), and click Start-up Scripts.

2. Do perform any of the following operation:

   - Select or deselect the desired scripts.

   - To enable or disable all scripts, click Enable All or Disable All.

- Click on Reveal My Start-up Scripts to go to Adobe Bridge Start-up Scripts folder on your hard drive.

- SPECIAL FEATURE- You can Work in Compact mode:

- You can switch to the Compact mode when you want to shrink the Adobe Bridge window. In Compact mode, the panels remain hidden and the Content panel is simplified. A subset of common Adobe Bridge commands remains available from the pop-up menu in the upper-right corner of the window.

- By default, the Compact mode window of Adobe Bridge floats on top of all windows. (In Full mode, the Adobe Bridge window can move behind other windows.) This floating window is useful because it is always available as you work in different applications.

- For instance, use Compact mode after you select the files you plan to use, and then drag them into this application as per your needs. You can Deselect Compact Window Always on Top from the Adobe

Bridge window menu to prevent the Compact mode Adobe Bridge window from floating on top of all windows. The instructions are as follows-

- Click the Switch to 'Compact Mode' button.

- Do perform any of the following:

- Choose commands from the menu at the upper-right corner of the Adobe Bridge window.

- Click the Switch to Ultra Compact Mode button to hide the Content panel, further minimizing the Adobe Bridge window. You can click on the same button again in order to return to the Compact mode.

- Click the Switch to Full Mode button to return to Full mode, displaying the panels, and letting Adobe Bridge move behind the current window.

How to manage color:

In Adobe Bridge, the quality of thumbnail determines whether the color profile settings are used or not.

The high-quality thumbnails use color-profile settings, while quick thumbnails do not. You may use the Advanced Preferences and the Options for Thumbnail Quality and Preview Generation button in the application bar to determine thumbnail quality.

If you are a Creative Cloud member or you own Adobe Creative Suite, you can use Adobe Bridge to synchronize the color settings across all color-managed apps and components.

When you specify the color settings using the Edit -> Color Settings (Bridge CC) or Edit -> Creative Suite Color Settings (Bridge CS) command, color settings automatically synchronize.

Synchronization of the color settings ensures that colors look the same in all color-managed Adobe products.

How to restore the preferences in the workspace:

There are various program settings stored in the Adobe Bridge preferences file, including display, Adobe Photo Downloader, performance, and file-handling options. These preferences can be restored to the workspace through the under-given procedure-

Restoring of the preferences returns settings to their defaults and it can often correct unusual application behavior.

The set of instructions are as follows-

1. Press and hold the Ctrl key (in Windows) or the Option key (in Mac OS) while starting Adobe Bridge.

2. In the Reset Settings dialog box, you can select one or more of the following options:

   Reset Preferences Returns preferences to their factory defaults. Some labels and ratings may be lost. Adobe Bridge creates a new preferences file when it starts. Purge Entire Thumbnail Cache Purging the thumbnail cache can help if Adobe Bridge is not displaying thumbnails properly. Adobe Bridge re-creates the thumbnail cache when it starts. Reset Standard Workspaces Returns Adobe predefined workspaces to their factory default configurations.

3. Click OK, or click Cancel to open the Adobe Bridge without resetting preferences.

How can you change the language settings?

Adobe Bridge displays the menus, options, and tool tips in different languages. You can also specify that Adobe Bridge use a specific language for keyboard shortcuts.

1. Choose Edit > Preferences (Windows) or Adobe Bridge > Preferences (Mac OS), and click Advanced.

2. Do perform either or both of the following:

    • You can choose a language from the Language menu to display menus, options, and tools tips in that language.

    • You can also choose a language from the Keyboard menu to use that language keyboard configuration for keyboard shortcuts.

3. Click OK, and restart the Adobe Bridge. The new language takes effect from the next time you start Adobe Bridge.

How can you compare and preview the images in Adobe Bridge:

Read the topic carefully to understand the very essential concept of previewing and comparing the images. The concept is highly useful for the designers and photographers.

You can preview images in Adobe Bridge in Preview panel, in Full Screen Preview as well as in Review mode. The Preview panel displays up to nine thumbnail images for quick comparisons. 'Full Screen Preview' displays images in full screen mode. Review mode displays images in a full-screen view that lets you navigate the images. It also lets you refine your selection, label, ratify, rotate image and open images in Camera Raw.

Procedure to View images as a slide show:

The Slideshow command lets you view thumbnails as a slide show that takes over the entire screen. It is an easy way to work with large versions of all the graphics files in a folder. You can pan and zoom images during a slide show, and set options that control slide show display, including transitions and captions.

The instructions are as follows-

- To view any slide show, you can open a folder of images, or select all the images you want to view in the slide show, and choose View -> Slideshow.

- To display all the commands for working with slide shows, press H while in Slideshow view.

- To specify slide show options, press 'L' while in Slideshow view, or, choose View -> Slideshow Options.

Display options: Choose these options to black out additional monitors, repeat the slide show, or zoom back and forth.

Slide options: these options specify the slide duration, captions, and slide scaling.

Transition options: These options specify the transition styles and speed.

Preview images using the Preview panel:

Now, understand the concept of previewing and comparing separately. The instruction set for previewing the images in the preview panel are as follows-

Select up to nine images from the Content panel and, if necessary, choose Window -> Preview Panel.

To preview images using the Full Screen Preview, follow-

- Select one or more images and choose View -> Full Screen Preview, or press the spacebar.

- Press the plus sign (+) or minus sign (-) key to zoom in or out of the image, or click the image to zoom to that point. You can also use a mouse scroll wheel to increase and decrease magnification.

- To pan the image, you can zoom in and then drag.

- Press the Right Arrow and Left Arrow keys to go to next and previous images in the folder. Note that, if you select multiple images before entering Full Screen Preview, by pressing the Right Arrow and Left Arrow keys cycles through the selected images.

- Press the spacebar or Esc to exit Full Screen Preview.

How to evaluate and select images using Review mode:

Review mode is full-screen view for browsing a selection of photos, refining the selection, and performing basic editing. It is a completely dedicated view. Review mode helps to display the images in a rotating carousel that you can navigate.

Review mode:

1. Open a folder of images or select the images you want to review and choose View > Review Mode.

2. Do perform any of the following operation:

    •   Click on the Left or Right Arrow buttons in the lower-left corner of the screen, or you can press the Left Arrow or Right Arrow key on your keyboard, in order to go to the previous or next image.

    •   You can drag the foreground image left or right to bring the previous or next image forward.

    •   You may click any image in the background to bring it to the front.

- Then, drag any image off the bottom of the screen to remove it from the selection, or click the Down Arrow button in the lower-left corner of the screen.

- Do right-click in Windows or Control-click in Mac OSon any image in the workspace to rate it, apply a label, rotate it, or open it.

- Press ']' to rotate the foreground image 90° clockwise, press '[' to rotate the image 90° counterclockwise.

- Press the Esc or click the 'X' button in the lower-right corner of the screen to exit Review mode.

- Click on the New Collection button in the lower-right corner of the screen to create a collection from the selected images and exit Review mode. Press H while in Review mode to display keyboard shortcuts for working in Review mode.

Ways to preview dynamic media files in Adobe Bridge:

You can preview most of the video and audio files in Adobe Bridge easily. You can also preview SWF, FLV, and F4V files as well as most files supported by the version of QuickTime you have sometime installed on your computer.

Instructions on how to preview the media files in the Preview panel-

1. Firstly, select the file to preview in the Content panel.

2. In the Preview panel, click on the Play button to start the video, click the Pause button to pause playback, click the Loop button to turn continuous loop on or off, or click the Volume button to adjust loudness.

You can brighten or darken the Adobe Bridge interface to better preview dynamic media files. See Adjust brightness and colors.

Play full-screen previews of dynamic media files

1. Select the file to preview in the Content panel.

2. Choose View > Full Screen Preview.

3. Click on the Pause button to pause playback, click on the Play button to resume playback, click the Loop button to turn continuous loop on or off, or click the Volume button to adjust loudness.

4. Press Esc to return to Adobe Bridge.

How can you set the playback preferences?

The playback preferences can be set according to the following of these instructions-

1. In Adobe Bridge, do choose Edit -> Preferences (in Windows).

2. Click on Playback.

3. Change any of the following settings, and click OK.

Know about Stack Playback Frame Rate:

In those stacks that contain 10 or more images, you can preview the images. This option lets you specify a frame rate for previewing image stacks.

How to play the Audio Files Automatically When Previewed:

When you click any audio file for a display in the Preview panel, audio begins to play automatically. Turn off the option to play audio files manually only.

How to loop the Audio Files When Previewed:

To continually repeat or loop the audio file, select loop option. You may deselect this option if you want the audio file to play only once.

How to play Video Files Automatically When Previewed:

It helps to play a video file automatically in the Preview panel when you select it in the Content panel.

How to loop Video Files When Previewed:

To continually repeat or loop the video file, select loop video option. You may deselect this option if you want the video file to play only once.

How to stack files in Adobe Bridge:

Stacks help you group different files together under a single thumbnail. You can stack any type of files together. For example, you may use stacks to organize image sequences, which often comprise many image files.

Note that, Adobe Bridge stacks are different from Photoshop image stacks, which convert groups of images to layers and store them in a Smart Object. Commands that apply to a single file also apply to stacks. For example, you can label a stack just as you would a single file. Commands you apply to expanded stacks apply to all files in the stack.

Commands you apply to collapsed stacks apply only to the top file in the stack, if you have selected only the top file in the stack or to all files in the stack, if you have selected all files in the stack by clicking the stack border. The default sort order in a stack relies on the sort order for the folder that contains the stack.

Ways to create file stack:

Select the files you want to include in the stack, and choose Stacks -> Group as Stack. The first file you select becomes the stack thumbnail. The number on the stack indicates how many files are in the stack.

Ways to manage the stacks:

- To change the stack thumbnail, right-click (in Windows) or Control-click (in Mac OS) the file you want to be the new thumbnail and choose Stacks -> Promote to Top of Stack.

- To expand a collapsed stack, click on the stack number or choose Stacks -> Open Stack. To expand all stacks, choose Stacks > Expand All Stacks.

- To collapse an expanded stack, click the stack number or choose Stacks -> Close Stack. To collapse all stacks, choose Stacks > Collapse All Stacks.

- To add files to a stack, drag the files you want to add to the stack. Note that, while you can add a stack to another stack, you cannot nest stacks.

- To remove files from a stack, expand the stack and then drag the files out of the stack. To remove all files from a stack, select the collapsed stack and choose Stacks -> Ungroup from Stack.

- To select all files in a collapsed stack, click the border of the stack. Alternatively, Alt-click (in Windows) or Control + click (in Mac OS) the stack thumbnail.

Ways to preview the images in stacks:

In stacks containing 10 or more images, you can always preview the images at a specified frame rate and enable onion skinning, which allows you to see preceding and succeeding frames as semi-transparent overlays on the current frame.

- To preview the stack, hold the mouse over the stack in the Content panel until the slider appears, and then click Play, or drag the slider. If you do not see the Play button or slider, increase the thumbnail size by dragging the Thumbnail slider at the bottom of the Adobe Bridge window.

- To set a playback frame rate, right click (in Windows) or Control-click (in Mac OS), on the stack and choose a frame rate from the Stacks > Frame Rate menu.

- To seta 'default stack playback frame rate', choose a frame rate from the Stack Playback Frame Rate menu in Playback preferences.

- To enable onion skinning, right-click (in Windows) or Control-click (in Mac OS), the stack and choose Stack -> Enable Onion Skin.

How to use collections in the Adobe Bridge:

Collections are an easy way to group photos in one place for easy and simple viewing, even if they are located in different folders or on different hard drives. 'Smart collections' are type of collection generated from a saved search. The Collections panel allows us to create, locate, and open collections, as well as create and edit smart collections.

Ways to create any collection:

Do perform any of the following operation:

- Click on the New Collection button at the bottom of the Collections panel to create a new, empty collection.

- Select one or more files in the Content panel and then click the New Collection button in the Collections panel. Click 'Yes' when asked if you want to include the selected files in the new collection.

By default, if you select a file in a collection, the file is list as being located in the collection folder. To navigate to the folder in which the file is physically located, select the file and then choose File >Reveal in Bridge.

Ways to create the smart collection:

Click on the New Smart Collection button at the bottom of the Collections panel.

To add or remove a smart collection from the Favorites panel, right-click (in Windows) or Control-click (in Mac OS), the smart collection in the Collections panel and choose 'Add to Favorites option' or 'Remove from Favorites option'.

Ways to edit a smart collection:

1. Select a smart collection in the Collections panel.

2. Click the 'Edit Smart Collection button'.

3. Do specify the new criteria for the smart collection, and then click Save. Note: Remove photos from a smart collection by editing the criteria.

Deleting a photo, while viewing a smart collection moves the photo to the Recycle Bin (Windows) or Trash (Mac OS).

Ways to rename a collection:

Do perform any of the following:-

- Double-click on the collection name and type a new name.

- Right-click (in Windows) or Control-click (in Mac OS) on the collection name and choose the Rename from the menu. Then, overwrite the name of the collection

Ways to delete a collection:

When you delete any collection, you simply remove it from collections list in the Adobe Bridge. No files are deleting from your hard disk.

To delete a collection, do perform any of the following operation:

- In the Collections panel, do select a collection name, and then click on the trash icon.

- Right-click (Windows) or Control-click (Mac OS) on a collection name, and then choose the Delete from the menu.

Ways to add files to any collection:

To add files to a collection, do perform any of the following:

- Do drag the files from the Content panel, the Explorer (Windows), or the Finder (Mac OS) to the collection name in the Collections panel.

- Do Copy and paste files from the Content panel onto a collection name in the Collections panel.

Ways to remove files from a collection:

To remove files from a collection, do select the collection in the Collections panel and do any of the following:-

- Select any file in the Content panel and click 'Remove from Collection', or right-click (Windows) or Control-click (Mac OS) and choose 'Remove from Collection'.

- Select a file in the Content panel and press Delete. Click Reject to mark the file as rejected, Delete to move it to the Recycle Bin (Windows) or the Trash (Mac OS), or Cancel to keep the file.

Instructions to copy files between collections-

1.   Select a collection in the Collections panel.

2.   Drag a file from the Content panel to the collection in the Collections panel that you want to copy.

Ways to locate the missing files:

Adobe Bridge tracks the locations of the files in collections. If a file is being moved in Adobe Bridge, the file remains in the collection too. If collection includes files that have been moved or renamed in the Explorer (Windows) or the Finder (Mac OS), or if the files are on a removable hard drive that is not connected when you view any collection, the Adobe Bridge displays alert at the top of the Content panel indicating that files are missing.

1. Click Fix to locate the missing files.

2. In the 'Find Missing Files' dialog box, select the missing files and do any of the following:-

- Click on Browse to navigate to the new location of the files.

- Click on Skip to ignore the missing files.

- Click on Remove to remove the missing files from the collection.

Methods of using keywords in Adobe Bridge:

The keyword panel is a very commonly used and important feature to go through. It includes creating of the new keywords, adding them to files and many other operations. The various operations in detail are in a list below.

How to create some new keywords or sub-keywords:

1. In the Keywords panel, select any keyword. For example, if Names is selected, adding of a new keyword creates a keyword on the same level as Names, such as Sports; and adding a new sub-keyword makes you create a keyword under various names.

2. Click the New Keyword button or New Sub Keyword button or choose either New Keyword or New Sub Keyword from panel menu.

3. Type the keyword name and press Enter (Windows) or Return (Mac OS). If you want a parent keyword to be used for structural purposes only, place the keyword in brackets, such as [Names]. Keywords in brackets cannot be added to the files.

You can also add keywords by using the Find box at the bottom of the Keywords panel. Use commas to indicate sub-keywords and semicolons to indicate separate entries.

How to add keywords to the files:

1. Select the file or files to ones you want to add keywords.

1. 2 In Keywords panel, select that box next to the name of the keyword or sub-keyword. Shift + click the box to select all parent keywords. A check mark appears in the box next to the keyword when it is added to a selected file. If you select multiple files, but the keyword was added to only some of

192

them, a hyphen (-) appears in the keyword box. Note: If you Shift-click a sub-keyword, the parent keywords are also added to the file. To change the behavior so that clicking a sub-keyword automatically adds the parent keywords (and Shift-clicking adds only the sub-keyword), select Automatically Apply Parent Keywords in Keywords preferences.

How to remove keywords from any file:

- To remove the check mark, do select the file, and then click on the box next to the name of the keyword or keyword set. For removing the 'check mark' from all parent keywords, Shift-click the keyword box.

- To remove a check mark forcibly, Alt-click (Windows) or Option-click (Mac OS) the keyword box. This method is useful when you select multiple files to which the keyword was applied, only to some, causing a hyphen to appear in the keyword box. To remove a 'check mark' from a keyword and its parents, do press Alt+Shift (Windows) or Option+Shift (Mac OS) and click the keyword box.

- Select the file, and then choose Remove Keywords from the Keywords panel menu. To remove all keywords from the file, click 'Yes'.

Lesson 10: Photoshop and The world of Vectors

When you utilize Adobe Photoshop to make design for your business and its customers, your symbolism comprises of pixels, minor square components that make up the gridded mosaic basic bitmapped pictures. Photoshop likewise bolsters vector, or way based, components, including live sort and different types of symbolism. When you need to change over a bitmapped component to vector ways, you can utilize a few strategies to make components more reminiscent of a drawing system like Adobe Illustrator than of a picture editorial manager like Photoshop.

Step 1

Press "P" to choose the Pen device. Open the "Window" menu and pick "Ways" to uncover the Paths board. In the Options bar, pick the standard form of the Pen apparatus to draw Bezier bends and exact straight lines, the freeform adaptation to make an inexactly drawn result reminiscent of pen on paper, or the Magnetic Pen to draw taking after the sharp moves of shading or brilliance in your picture. Draw your vector ways so they speak to a followed transformation of the components of your picture.

Press "Enter" to flag the end of a way, open or shut, or click on the opening stay point to finish your way where it began.

Step 2

Make a choice utilizing any mix of the Marquee, Magic Wand, Lasso and other determination devices. To transform your determination into a way, open the flyout menu at the upper right corner of the Paths board and pick "Make Work Path," or snap on the relating catch at the base of the board. Set a resilience worth to administer how firmly or freely your way takes after your unique determination's limits. At 0.5 pixels, your way safeguards unpretentious movements in your determination, though at 10 pixels, your way utilizes few stay focuses and showcases smooth moves.

Step 3

Double tap on the Work Path that shows up in the Paths board when you first draw with the Pen instrument or proselyte a choice to a way. Name your way or acknowledge the default "Way [X]," where "[X]" speaks to a number. Unless you change over your Work Path to a named way, the following move you make that makes a way will supplant the vector drawing on your current Work Path with new vector yield.

Step 4

Send out a way from your Photoshop record in Adobe Illustrator AI configuration to use in different projects. Open the "Record" menu, find its "Fare" submenu and pick "Ways to Illustrator." The subsequent document contains ways without any strokes or fills.

Tips

Shape layers comprise of a load with a vector veil that characterizes the edge of the shape. On the off chance that you select the Pen apparatus and snap on the "Shape Layers" catch in the Options bar, the subsequent vector drawing structures the cover for a shape.

When you change over a determination to a way, any halfway straightforward edges turn out to be hard-edged moves.

You can change a way the same way you would change a completely or incompletely chose picture layer. Utilize the "Way Selection" device to choose all or a piece of the vector component you need to change. Open the "Alter" menu, find its "Change Path" submenu and pick the change you need to apply, including Free Transform or any of its part changes, for example, Warp or Rotate.

Lesson 11: Text

You can likewise include content in Photoshop and confirm qualities, for example, the textual style, size and shade of the content. Remember that the primary motivation behind why individuals make content in Photoshop is to add a visual component to their Photoshop picture with short messages as opposed to sort out long sections or make content just reports.

There are various preferences to vector sort. For instance, when printed with a PostScript yield gadget, the edges stay fresh and clean, without the supposed jaggies—the unmistakable stair-step edges of pixels along a bend. Vector fine art can be scaled in a representation program or by a PostScript printer and still hold those amazing edges. Since it comprises of numerically characterized ways, it can likewise be controlled in courses outlandish with raster workmanship. Figure below looks at broadened vector and raster characters and shows how the vector ways of an individual character may be altered.

The essential point of interest of raster workmanship is its capacity of duplicating fine moves and degrees in shading, for example, those found in photos. Since sort is typically solitary shading, that ability is not of specific worth. Be that as it may, Photoshop's vector sort can be rasterized when essential.

The contrast in the middle of vector and rasterized sort is fundamentally of significance amid the creation procedure and when gets ready work of art for arrangement in a page design program. In most different circumstances, the sort is consequently rasterized. Keep in mind that Web fine art arranged in Photoshop is raster (counting any content fused into the pictures). Moreover, inkjet printers don't exploit vector sort. (Just PostScript printers can really work with vectors in that capacity.) When yielding to an inkjet printer, sparing pictures for the Web, or utilizing a non-PostScript record arrangement, sort is consequently rasterized. This doesn't mean, in any case, that you need to rasterize the sort physically. Rather, abandon it as vector in your unique report with the goal that it can be altered, and let the printer's product rasterize upon yield.

The improved TIFF document configuration can likewise bolster vector sort layers, yet full usage of the position's propelled components aside from the Adobe Creative Suite is for all intents and purposes nonexistent.

At the point when sparing in a configuration that can keep up vector fine art or sort, you'll have to guarantee that the Include Vector Data alternative is chosen. You'll see check confines the different PostScript document design alternatives dialog boxes (this show up after Photoshop's Save As option box). While EPS and DCS alternative dialog boxes caution about reviving records in the Photoshop and the PDF option dialog box will not.

One more point of interest of utilizing vector sort as a part of Photoshop is sort twisting. Tapping the Warp kind of catch in the Options Bar permits you to look over a mixture of preset (yet adaptable) sort mutilation alternative.

Lesson 12: Output and Automation

Bunch handling is valuable when you have a great deal of pictures that require the same activities to be connected to them. With a couple key strokes you can rapidly "transform" a whole envelope of pictures.

We'll utilize the activity we made in the Actions lesson obviously you can utilize your own particular or simply take after along.

STEP 1: Getting Started

I have an organizer of full measured pictures that should be changed over to thumbnails. I additionally need them to have a drop shadow connected to them and have them changed over to .gif to use on my site. I've officially made my activity to transform every picture, except I definitely don't have a craving for experiencing every picture and applying the activity it.

STEP 2: Applying the Settings

Begin by going to File>Automate>Batch...

In the Play choice, select which Set contains the activity you need to apply. In this illustration, "CBT Cafe" is the Set I chose.

Pick the Action to apply. I just have one in this set and it's called: Thumbnails 75x50 w/drop shadow. On the off chance that I had more activities in this Set they would be noticeable starting from the drop menu.

In the Source choice, pick Folder starting from the drop menu and afterward tap the Choose... catch to explore to the envelope containing your pictures.

For Destination select Folder starting from the drop menu. Another choice I often use for Destination is the None choice. By selecting None, Photoshop applies the activity to the pictures however leaves the pictures open. This is useful in the event that I need to see my new pictures and figure out whether I have to make any further alters to them. For this sample, on the other hand, we'll choose an envelope.

After you select the Folder choice, snap Choose... to choose your destination envelope. You can choose a present envelope or you can make another one. I'll make another one called Output on my Desktop.

The following alternative, Override Action "Save As" Commands, ought to be chosen if your activity contains a "Spare As..." or "Put something aside for Web..." charge. In the event that your activity doesn't contain a "Spare As..." summon you'll have to keep this alternative unchecked to spare your records. Photoshop will provoke you to spare every record when this choice is not chose. For my illustration I'll choose the choice since I have a "Put something aside for Web..." order in my activity.

Select a File Naming tradition for your pictures. I for the most part utilize lowercase names and select the second choice starting from the drop menu. The last alternative I regularly select is for Errors: Stop for Errors. This is exceptionally useful for troubleshooting your orders.

* 9 7 8 1 5 1 7 5 9 8 1 9 8 *